D0007316

peace+love

peace + love
janet lynn

with Dean Merrill

Creation House
Carol Stream, Illinois

© 1973 by Creation House. All rights reserved
Printed in the United States of America
Published by Creation House,
499 Gundersen Drive, Carol Stream, Illinois 60187

First printing: 50,000

International Standard Book Number 0-88419-069-2
Library of Congress Catalog Card Number 73-89731

contents

1

going around in circles

I had made my decision even before we left Sapporo. In a quiet corner of the Olympic press quarters I told my mother, "I've got to go on. I know it's been a long thirteen years of skating, and I'm tired. But I'm going to skate another year. Maybe even to the next Olympics."

Down underneath, she was wishing I would quit. She'd been my travel agent, chauffeur, seamstress, secretary, and constant companion all over the world while trying to be a wife and mother of four at the same time. We'd built everything these last years toward Sapporo. And the competition had been so wild for me: messing up badly on a compulsory school figure, then winning the bronze medal with my free skating—in spite of falling once.

And there I stood, saying we weren't yet finished. I had to defend my national title for a fourth time, and compete once again at the 1973 world championships in Bratislava, Czechoslovakia.

1

All she said was, "Well, if that's what you want, we're behind you."

I had already told the Lord, "It seems like You want me to skate another year for You. You know I don't want to; You know I'm tired of it. So I'll just have to trust You for the strength to make it."

At first it was fairly easy. The first morning back home in Rockford, Illinois, I was awakened by the flash of a newspaper photographer's camera taking a picture of me sleeping. I got up and began facing the euphoria of being an Olympic medalist. There were six big boxes of gifts from Japanese fans to unpack—everything from dolls and a flute to a black karate belt and some fencing gear! I especially loved a hand-embroidered wedding kimono given to me by a junior-high-age boy and his father one day while I had been practicing in Sapporo. The boy had claimed it was worth over three hundred dollars; it must have belonged to his mother.

The incoming mail each day was mountainous. We finally just gave George Szuminski, our postman, a key to the house so he could come in and unload it if we weren't home. My grandpa began the job of sorting it out; many of the letters were in Japanese, which a foreign-exchange student at Guilford translated for us.

A special Janet Lynn festival was held over the Mother's Day weekend. A big bunch of skaters came in to help me do five exhibitions at the Wagon Wheel Ice Palace—Suna Murray, Dorothy Hamill, Gordie McKellen, Melissa and Mark Militano, and others. John B. Anderson, our congressman, came to the dinner.

The next Thursday night I was in Birmingham to talk briefly at a Billy Graham crusade. It was a huge "youth night" crowd—fifty-six thousand—and I told them, "I'd never have won the bronze medal this year without Jesus."

The honors just kept coming. I couldn't believe all this was happening to me—things like being on the cover of *Ingenue* in June, and a trip back to Japan not to skate but to attend the premiere of a film about the Olympics. I'd never been surrounded by so many photographers in my life.

In fact, I was enjoying everything but skating. A lady came

2

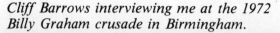

*Cliff Barrows interviewing me at the 1972
Billy Graham crusade in Birmingham.*

up to me with her little girl one day while I was changing
skates in the lobby of the rink. She asked if I were Janet Lynn,
and I said yes.

"Oh, my daughter just loves you!" she began gushing. "She
likes to skate, too, and she watches you every time you're on
TV, and she wants to be just like you some day."

At this, the little girl broke into tears and began screaming,
"No I don't, mommy, no I don't!"

She was smarter than she knew; in a way I hope she never
goes through a skating year like I was into right then. It was
becoming the worst year of my life. The longer I skated, the
more I hated it. I had never been so tempermental on the ice.

3

Part of me was really disturbed by how I felt. "I've always loved skating," I told myself. "Why am I sick of something that has brought me so much joy and fulfillment?"

I didn't really get very far praying about it. I had given God permission to run my life, but now I didn't like what He had done with it. He'd led me to skate one more year, and the grind was driving me out of my mind. Every day, six days a week, skating from eight or eight-thirty in the morning to four in the afternoon . . . I felt like I was wasting my life away doing nothing but going around in circles in an ice rink.

I kept struggling through the hot weeks. I couldn't care less about defending my national title in Minneapolis the next January or going to Bratislava or anything . . . in fact, I dreaded it to the very bottom of my tired, overweight legs.

Finally, about the middle of August, I got on the ice one morning and said, "This is ridiculous. I'm hating every minute. I don't know why I'm doing this; I don't even know if it's the Lord's will for me or not. If it is, why am I hating it so much?"

Within ten minutes, I came off the rink, took off my skates, and drove back home. I walked in the house and announced to a shocked mother, "Mom, I'm going to quit skating. I can't stand it any more."

If only I could have been a little girl again . . . .

My dad was probably the only "den father" in the history of Cub Scouting.

It wasn't that he had Wednesday afternoons free when the Cub Scout pack met. But my mom, the official den mother, was too busy even back then—teaching Sunday school, making costumes for school plays, serving as a room mother at school, taking care of a family—and a basement-full of rowdy boys (including my older brothers Larry, six, and Glenn, five) got to be a little too much. Especially with me, a two-year-old, wanting her attention at all the wrong times.

So by the winter of 1955, my dad was leaving his drug store at 83rd and Kedzie on the southwest side of Chicago to come home and run the pack meeting once a week. Doctors in Chicago took Wednesdays off back then, so there weren't

4

as many prescriptions to fill anyway. He made a great "den father"—the boys did more woodworking and rope-tying than they ever would have with my mother!

One day my dad said, "How would you kids like to go skating some Saturday?" The response was a loud "Yeah!" Most of them already had skates. The one person without skates was me. Of course my folks could have left me with a baby-sitter—but that's something they almost never did. They had the philosophy that families should enjoy things together, that for the first twenty years or so of their marriage they should get most of their kicks out of doing things *with* their kids instead of apart from them.

So when the Saturday came and the pond was frozen, little Janet went along with the Cub Scouts. My mom had driven all over the city before she found a pair of skates small enough for me.

I was much too young to remember that day, but my parents tell me that I found skating to be about the neatest thing since graham crackers. Larry and Glenn propped me up at first, but soon I was trying—and falling—all by myself. My mom expected that the first fall would send me crying into her arms, but for some reason I thought it was funny. I'd laugh; when anyone tried to help me up, I'd say, "Me do it *me*-self!"

The Cub Scouts went skating often that winter, and before long I'd taught myself how to skate backwards by watching the other kids on the pond. This sounds like I was terribly aggressive and brave—but the truth is that down underneath I was the most shy of all the Nowicki children. At that age I was especially petrified by men—even our neighbors or my own uncle. When mom had first started me in dancing classes, I would sit at her feet through the entire lesson and refuse to get up and try anything. At home I'd practice all the steps, but for the first two months I wouldn't do a thing in class.

And maybe that's one of the reasons why, all through childhood, I kept working at my skating: I was too embarrassed to have anyone see a mistake. The very thought of my skating teachers, my parents, or anyone watching me skate poorly often drove me toward perfection.

Skating was no big thing at first; my parents held no cherished dreams that someday I'd be an Olympic star, and neither

Larry and Glenn with me in my first skating outfit—
red velvet with white satin trim. I was 3½.

did I. I can't say skating was—or has ever been—the sole driving passion of my life. It's been a fun thing, a talent given me to develop, and I've worked to make the most of my gift. But that has not eliminated the many other interests of a girl growing up.

By the next year, when I was 3½, Mom enrolled all three of us at the Michael Kirby Ice Skating School on Loomis Boulevard. I still have, in a scrapbook, a sales check dated November 12, 1956, for a size 11 pair of Hyde figure skates. They cost $11.28. My folks paid $6.28 that day and had to put the skates in layaway until they could get the remaining $5.00. (It's good they didn't know that someday they'd be paying $150 a pair for custom-made skates!)

Size 11 was far too big—the tops came almost to my knees. But for some reason they were the smallest available, and so I just wore extra pairs of socks. My first teacher was a young woman named Stephanie Brosius, and I had a good time in class. At the end of that season came the special Ice Carnival, when all the Michael Kirby students would do their thing in front of parents and friends downtown at the big Chicago Stadium.

The night arrived—April 21, 1957. The printed program had my name misspelled ("Janet Norwicki"). Along with ten others in the Advanced Tiny Tots class, I was supposed to do a simple number called "Easter Parade." We girls all wore dressy dresses and Easter bonnets and carried big straw baskets with flowers.

I took one look out onto that ice . . . that absolutely huge stadium, home of the Black Hawks hockey team, with its 16,666 seats . . . and began to cry hysterically. I was scared to death. Another little girl named Debbie took my hand and said, "Come on, Janet, it won't hurt." She succeeded in dragging me onto the ice.

Thus began my performance career!

Once I got out there, I forgot my fear and did all right.

Glenn got to be dressed up as an umpire for something called "Casey at the Bat" that night; Larry missed the show because of appendicitis. The truth is that both of them never were serious about skating; they kept getting kicked out of classes for goofing off. I almost quit, too, the next October when suddenly Stephanie Brosius wasn't there one week . . . she had been replaced by a *man*! His name was Dick Rasmussen. He was very nice and all that, but I still went flying off the ice the first time I saw him. It took a full month for my mom to talk me into going back.

My earliest memories, of course, are of our neighborhood on South Millard Avenue (actually, we lived in the suburb of

Evergreen Park, which is surrounded on three sides by Chicago) . . . the park down at the end of the block . . . the little red-haired girl across the street I always used to fight with . . . the hours of playing and practicing my gymnastics lessons in the sandbox made by my Grandpa Gehrke . . . my brothers and Brian Thelander, the kid next door, the three big bullies of the block . . . Brian's dad getting a big kick out of throwing everybody in their backyard swimming pool at neighborhood parties . . . praying every night at bedtime, "God, please let me have a sister" (He did—Carol was born when I was four.)

I remember how I always loved the rain . . . it felt so warm and soft . . . and how maddening it was always to have to go inside instead of staying out and enjoying it. The biggest thrill on summer evenings was for all of us kids to get into our pajamas—and then go outside and catch fireflies!

I remember Sunday school at Bethel Evangelical Lutheran Church—my dad was even the superintendent for a year. I cried the day his term of service came to an end. He had gone to a weeknight class to be better prepared, and I think it was around this time that my folks came to know Jesus Christ in a personal way.

When I started kindergarten at Central School in September 1958, I met the biggest scare of my life so far: fire drills! I would get absolutely hysterical. Long after we'd come back inside and all the other kids were quietly working, I would still be crying. One time I carried on so long that the school office had to call my mom to come and settle me down.

In January, I moved to a new level in skating: private lessons. A lady named Dodie Drallmier was my teacher at the Crystal Ice Rink. One day I saw a friend named Bibi Zillmer carefully going around in circles on the ice, and asked her what she was doing. She introduced me to what became my greatest challenge and my greatest frustration: school figures.

There are sixty-nine different patterns, all variations on the figure eight. The variations come from doing them on the left foot or the right foot using the forward or the back part of the skate on the inside or the outside edge of the blade . . . it gets rather complicated. The point is to trace the figure your second, third, fourth, fifth, and even sixth time around as closely as you can to the way you etched it on the ice the first time.

Anyway, I began trying. It wasn't nearly as much fun as whirling and leaping across the rink, but then, school figures were part of skating. I was so lightweight that sometimes at an outdoor rink the Chicago gusts would blow me right off the figure I was tracing.

At the same time, I kept up group lessons at the Michael Kirby school, this time with Peter Dunfield, (He's now a professional teacher in New York and has worked with the Olympic teams). He was very nice and patient, but also very strict about goofing around. For each class, we were supposed to write out what we'd learned the previous week. That was a little tough for me, since I was the youngest in the class and didn't know how to write yet. So I drew pictures instead (see next page).

By the time I was almost six, my third Ice Carnival came a-round and I got to do a solo. It even included a ballet jump. I really thought I was big stuff to have my picture, along with Kathy Beam, on the flyer promoting the show.

The solo went okay, I guess, but the group number had problems. At the end, the whole line was supposed to curtsy. Evidently, all the others forgot; they just stood there watching me curtsy all alone!

Among those adults who paid three dollars apiece to see two thousand little squirts skate around was my Grandma Gehrke. It was the last time she ever saw me skate. She'd had a hole in her heart for years, and it took quite a lot of effort for her to get to the stadium in her weakened condition. Two months later, she died, and not long after, grandpa moved in with us. He's been with us ever since, working behind the scenes washing dishes, cooking, sorting fan mail, and doing a thousand other jobs.

That summer we changed teachers again in order to get more personal attention and more ice time. Gladyce Jacobs was her name, and she taught at a skating school up in Park Ridge, northwest of the city near O'Hare Field. The school was really jammed, though; my "patch," (time to practice figures on a small square, or "patch," of ice) was 5:00-6:00

APRIL 12 - 1959

Left: *One of my first "reports" for Peter Dunfield's class.*
Above: *My costume for my 1959 Ice Carnival solo, when I was not quite six.*

A.M. on Saturday. That meant getting out of bed at three in the morning in order to get there on time!

But like my mother said to a sportswriter once, "What do you do when all a little girl ever says is, 'I wanna skate, I wanna skate, I wanna skate!'?"

2
the wagon wheel

Then came the day that changed everything. We had no idea what we were getting into that August Saturday when my family and I and Sue Ann Ready, a skating friend, drove up to Rockton, Illinois.

Rockton wasn't much—a sleepy little village of not more than two thousand people almost on the Wisconsin line. But it is the home of the Wagon Wheel, a large rustic resort built uniquely of logs and railroad ties. It has hotel space, restaurants, swimming pools, antique shops, a golf course, a riding stable, a bowling alley, a dinner theater . . . and an ice rink.

We'd heard in Chicago that there were some really good skaters and teachers at the Wagon Wheel; in fact, Dodie Drallmier had taken a bunch of her students up earlier in the summer, but Sue and I hadn't been able to go. We had all kinds of fun this Saturday, swimming, bowling, watching the candy kitchen, and just looking around. Then we kids went skating.

I remember looking out onto the ice and thinking, "Wow, such a big rink!" Up until then I'd been only on very small indoor studio rinks (in the summer) or larger but outdoor rinks (in the winter). This was so new and beautiful and the ice was really shiny and . . . then I saw this young woman teaching on the ice.

My mom and dad noticed her, too. Her student seemed to be totally absorbed in what she was saying, and there was a fire, a drive in the lady that fascinated us.

I kept watching her as I skated around. Pretty soon, my mom called me over to the edge. "Would you like to take a lesson from that lady?" she asked me.

"Sure!" I said.

"Okay, we'll see if she's willing," my mom replied. I went back to skating, and soon I saw my folks getting acquainted with Miss Slavka Kohout (pronounced "ka-*hoot*"), junior ladies' national runner-up in 1946, now manager and resident professional of the Wagon Wheel Ice Palace.

When they asked if she had time to give their little six-year-old daughter a quick lesson, Miss Kohout replied, "You mean you'll let me?" (She often uses that phrase.) We spent only fifteen minutes together, working on waltz jumps, three-turns, and single jumps—but when she talked, she had so much meaning in her voice. I'd never been so captivated in my life. My mom said later that listening made even her want to get up and skate!

We had discovered my last teacher.

Before the day was over, regular lessons had been set up. Miss Kohout insisted that I would need to come twice a week—Wednesdays and Saturday—if I wanted to get anywhere. I don't know if my parents gulped or not—they probably did. But they said okay. My mom went back to Evergreen Park and talked the school into letting me miss Wednesdays that fall in first grade (actually, kindergarten was the only normal year of school I ever had). She said, "Just give Janet a chance. If she can't keep up with her schoolwork, then I'll make her quit. But let's at least try it for a while." If she only knew how many times she'd be repeating that line!

When I look back on that day—and other "little" things

14

that happened—I really think God had it all planned. In fact, I know He did. So many things turned out to be important that didn't seem so at the time. I can't help believing that God knew what was going on and for some reason wanted me to skate.

Every Tuesday afternoon after school, either Mom or Dad or both would drive me the 100 Illinois Tollway miles to the Wagon Wheel. I'd skate that evening and all the next day, and then we'd drive the 100 miles back home that evening. On Fridays the whole family made the trip. We wouldn't be home again until late Sunday night. Every week was the same, all through the fall, winter and spring. Sometimes the snow would be so bad that half the local kids wouldn't even show up—but the Nowickis from Chicago were always there.

There's simply no way for me to thank my parents for all they poured into me. Even now, my mom tells people, "Well, we saw that Janet had a talent, and we just felt that we should do what we could to develop it. We *wanted* to. Her lessons with Miss Kohout just seemed like they were meant to be." I *know* that deep down underneath they must have dreaded that long trip sometimes. But I never felt any resistance from them.

Larry and Glenn, of course, had a great time skating and doing all the other things at the Wagon Wheel. They eventually even joined pee-wee hockey teams there. Dad got a part-time job in Rockford (fifteen miles away), since a pharmacist willing to work Saturdays and Sundays was always welcome. At least that was a better way to spend the weekend than sitting around shivering in an ice rink, and it helped pay for gasoline and tolls.

During my half-hour lessons with Miss Kohout, I was totally in awe of her, not only this first year but until I was at least nine or ten. I would never say a word to her except for a soft little yes or no when she asked me a question. She told my mom, "I never get a word out of her. All I get are those two big eyes gazing up at me, and then she goes out and does whatever I say!"

Recently in *Skating* magazine, Dick Button, the only American ever to win two gold medals in Olympic skating,

15

was interviewed. He said, "Most clubs are run by committees; but a sport like skating, which is in a certain sense an art form, requires—as does any theatrical enterprise— a dictator. Most clubs do not have a dictator in this sense, as does, for example, Rockton, Illinois, where Slavka Kohout sets the tone for the whole place."

True!

I joined the Wagon Wheel Figure Skating Club that year and got my membership in the United States Figure Skating Association. The USFSA has a series of eight tests —figures and steps—culminating in the gold figure test. (This was, incidentally, the only goal my parents ever suggested for me—they never pushed me in later years regarding the Olympics, world championships, or anything like that.) I passed the preliminary figure test on May 22, 1960, and Test No. 1 on July 30.

About that time, as I was finishing first grade, Miss Kohout had an interesting suggestion for my folks: "What would you think of dropping the name Nowicki as far as Janet's skating is concerned?" She was obviously looking forward to the day when I'd be in competition, and she lined up the following reasons for a change:

1. "Nowicki" is hard for some people to pronounce as well as spell.

2. It's hard to understand over a PA system during an ice show.

3. Skating is a very political sport with lots of unpredictable people, and let's not distract, say, a Russian judge someday with a Polish name on an American skater.

My folks agreed that on the ice, I could easily use my middle name and just be Janet Lynn. Later on, some Polish-American groups frowned on that, but it was probably still the wisest move for me.

The end of school meant the end of the tollway pilgrimages for a while—which was fine with me. It meant no more getting sick in the car, which is something all four of us kids were rather good at. (Up until three years ago,

16

I spent most airplane trips with my head in a sack! I've been Dramamine's best customer, I'm sure.) I enrolled in Miss Kohout's summer skating school which started near the end of June and ran to Labor Day.

In other words, my mom, Carol, and I simply moved to the Wagon Wheel, while dad, Larry, Glenn, and grandpa ran the house or else went fishing in northern Wisconsin. There were twenty-six of us in the school, and it was great to be on ice every day. I had three patch hours a day—9:00, 1:00, and 6:00—to work on figures, with the result that I passed USFSA Test No. 2 the day before the summer school ended.

I hadn't been back in second grade a month before Miss Kohout told my folks, "Look—if you want Janet to keep going in skating, we're just going to have to work out something for her to skate every day. This twice-a-week business is nothing but a standstill. Let me see if I can find a family here in the area with whom she could stay."

My parents, tired of the commuting, agreed with her. They said, "We'd like to move out of the city anyway—we have looked up around Barrington, and we've even talked about Colorado. But we can't do anything right away. Maybe on a temporary basis Janet could go up to Rockton, and we'll see what happens from there."

By October, the plans were set for me to move in with Jada Steinke (the girl we had first seen Miss Kohout teaching a year before) and her parents, who lived in Beloit, Wisconsin, three or four miles from Wagon Wheel.

It seemed hard to believe that what had started so innocently on a pond with a bunch of Cub Scouts had become so big. I, a pony-tailed seven-year-old, was leaving home.

3
first
competition

Jada was four years older than I, but we had a lot of fun together both on and off the ice. I especially remember sneaking into each other's rooms late at night to keep on talking after we were supposed to be asleep.

But then, when the lights were turned out and I tried to go to sleep, it was lonesome. Skating couldn't totally replace my family, whom I got to see only on weekends. My little mind kept churning, "I miss my mom and dad and everybody. It's fun to skate, but I want my mommy."

Soon my folks worked out a more permanent arrangement. My grandpa had had his second heart attack during the summer, but was feeling pretty good now. He went to his doctor on November 1 and said, "Before my wife died, she always said, 'If anything happens to me, you be sure and take good care of Janet' (that's my granddaughter, you know). What if I moved up to an apartment in Rockton and took care of her? She's a skater . . .".

18

The doctor cut him off. "Gus, that'd be the best thing you could do. It would keep you busy and useful—that's a great idea."

So before the month was out, my sixty-seven-year-old grandpa and I were settled in one of the Dutch Door one-bedroom apartments in Rockton, about a mile from the rink. I entered my third school in three months: Stephen Mack School. First, second, and third grades were all in one room.

Grandpa was a "good mother;" he'd get me up in the morning, brush my hair, fix me breakfast, then drive me to the rink. He'd even venture out onto the ice in his shoes to look at my figure tracings and try to coach me. Then he'd drive me to school, then back to the rink . . . and so it went.

The increase in skating time must have had an effect on my appetite. We always ate out in the evening at Dora's Diner, and my usual meal was a salad, a T-bone steak, a baked potato, a vegetable, a roll, something to drink, and a dessert! (In my defense, I have to say that my lunches were usually just peanut-butter-and-jelly sandwiches.)

Grandpa and I really got along pretty well. The one major problem was brushing my hair. Sometimes my pony tail would stay in for two weeks at a time. One day while he was brushing in back, I proceeded to even the score by carving up the front of his dresser with a knife! Don't think there wasn't something to discuss with my parents *that* weekend.

Meanwhile, Miss Kohout was getting her students ready for competition—the Midwestern sectional in Troy, Ohio, right after New Year's. On Christmas Day I saw my picture in a newspaper (the *Rockford Morning Star*) for the first time— not because I had any chance of winning, but because I was so young to be competing. We worked and worked on school figures, which at that time made up sixty percent of the total scoring. And we put together a free-skating program set to music, the ballet-type performance everyone is used to seeing on TV or in ice shows.

I didn't realize it at the time, of course, but figure skating is one of those few sports (along with gymnastics and diving) that can't be measured in a definite way. In baseball you either score a run or you don't; in track you run either faster or slower than the other person, and there's (usually!) no question about it. But in something artistic like skating, it's all up to human opinion—a panel of judges.

I read a description once in a newspaper column by Jim Murray:

> The school figures, a series of complicated arabesques . . . find the skaters writhing in semi-circles—now on one edge of the blade, now on the other.
>
> Judges come solemnly on ice, peer at these tracings like a hock-shop proprietor testing a ring for glass content, and then score the performance—six for perfect, zero for lousy. They require six judges because nobody trusts anybody in figure skating. It was a sport pioneered by rich people whose ego was at issue, not their sportsmanship.
>
> A judge who can spot a marking made by an inner blade versus one made by an outer edge qualifies to determine the sex of a gnat two blocks away . . . . Contestants do not hesitate to yell, "We wuz robbed" . . . .

It's true that a lot of people complain about the judging— they say, "How can you avoid partiality when the judges stand around and talk to the skaters and coaches during practice and even offer suggestions?" One sportswriter wrote, "This is the only sport where you can go out and do a perfect double lutz and get marked down for it because a judge saw you do a triple in practice."

But all in all, I have to say that I think *I* have been judged fairly—as fairly as human beings can judge something. I don't know if I could say that for every skater, but for myself I don't really have any gripes. Actually, I've never paid that much attention to the scores. My dad was always adding up the figures and computing the different factors and everything, but I guess I was always thinking more about the skating itself than the judging.

Anyway, at Troy I was entered in the juvenile ladies'

division. (There are five divisions now: juvenile, intermediate, novice, junior, and senior. Back then they didn't have intermediate.) I was the youngest competitor there, and my figures weren't all that hot; I came in thirteenth out of twenty. It really broke my heart, because you had to place in the top eight or else you couldn't free-skate. So I never got to do my program.

Naturally, I cried, and a news photographer took a picture of my dad kneeling down with his arm around me trying to comfort me, which went out on the Associated Press wire all over the country. (The caption, by the way, called him "Florian Lynn" instead of Florian Nowicki.)

The only good part was that Jada won the juvenile ladies' division. As for me, I got home and announced, "That's the last time I'm ever going to a competition without free-skating!" And it was, too.

In a way, it was good that I had to do figures. It taught me how to discipline myself more than if I had been free-skating only. There were so many times during patch that I'd be going around my figures and my mind would be miles away. I couldn't care less about what I was doing; I'd suddenly start singing a song I'd heard on the radio or something!

But then there would be other times when I would really concentrate. I'd really work at it, and when I couldn't do it right, I'd get frustrated. And then my temper would flare up. My mom was watching patch one day, and I started kicking the ice, and she got *so mad*—all of a sudden, I wasn't on the ice anymore! She had picked me up by my pony tail and dragged me over the boards. She yelled, "Don't you ever show your temper on the ice like that again!"

I started crying. She told me not to get back on the ice, and then she left the rink! I didn't know where she went; I just sat there on the floor between the seats crying and crying and crying for I don't know how long.

That's how it went lots of times with figures—either I was daydreaming, or else I was getting frustrated. Once in a while, I would really be concentrating and my figures would be going really well, and I'd think, "This is fun; I really can do these things." And I'd concentrate so hard that my mind

My first competition in Troy, Ohio; I was a second-grader.

would start branching off into really deep thoughts on other subjects—and all of a sudden my figures were bad again.

There's still a lot of discussion in the skating world about whether being able to lay down six tracks within three or four inches is all that important. In another part of that interview in *Skating* magazine, Dick Button said,

> Figures are not the basis of free skating. They are not the scales on a piano.... They are a complete and separate entity, an art form in themselves which is a part of the overall sport.

It's fun and difficult to do them, and interesting; but they have little to do with free skating or improving free-skating technique.

A lot of people would disagree with him, of course. I don't really remember what I was told about figures at the beginning. For a long time I talked myself into the fact that they were the fundamentals and that if I got my figures better, my free skating would be better.

But I can say this much for school figures: at least I learned that in life there are some things you *have* to do even if you don't like them. You can teach yourself to like them well enough to do what you have to do. I don't see any other way I could have learned to discipline myself so much.

4
"she just needs time"

The rest of the year with grandpa went well, and I finished second grade. I got to be in a couple of special exhibitions at the Wagon Wheel and also up at Lake Geneva, Wisconsin.

By the time school was out, my dad had sold his half of the drug store in Chicago, and everyone moved to Rockford. He lost quite a bit of money on the sale and didn't go back into business for himself until seven years later. Instead he became the manager of the drug store where he'd been working weekends. We moved into a partly unfinished house on Marsh Avenue out on Rockford's northeast side.

It was great to be back together as a family once again. After so much running and traveling on the weekends we got back in church on a regular basis. We settled at Gloria Dei Lutheran Church, which had been started just four years earlier. They didn't have a permanent sanctuary yet, and it used to get really hot sitting on those folding chairs in the summer.

But there was one day that I'll never forget. Pastor Peterson said something in his sermon—I don't remember what—that really struck me. Grade-school kids spend a lot of church time daydreaming, I know, but once in a while they pay attention. And this day I was really hit by what he said, and I started crying right there in the middle of church.

I think I kept my folks from noticing; at least no one talked about it afterwards. But for the next several weeks I began thinking—really thinking—about the Lord's Prayer when I said it each night before bed. I'd always just rattled it off really fast, but I started thinking, "Why do I say that prayer? I don't even know what it means."

So the first night, I prayed, "Our Father, who art in heaven—" and stopped. What does that mean? Father . . . that's pretty personal. But it says He's in heaven. So He is a close and personal Father even though He's in heaven.

I went on: "Hallowed be Thy name." What does that mean? It means God's name is blessed and really sacred.

Eventually I got all the way through the Lord's Prayer figuring out its true meaning. Then each time I prayed it I tried to think about the meanings I had decided on instead of just reciting a bunch of words. This was one of the first steps of my growth in faith even though I hadn't actually become a Christian yet.

The next years—third, fourth, fifth grades—were a happy combination of school each day sandwiched between an hour and a half of skating early in the morning and another 2½ hours in the late afternoon. Skating really challenged me. My dad would come to pick me up, and I'd say, "Just a little bit longer, okay?" I'd still be on the ice forty-five minutes later unless he said something.

My first full competition season was during third grade. Competition season is December through February. During those months there are four levels:

1. The *subsectionals* (these started in 1961 as more and

26

more kids got into skating). I was involved in the Upper Great Lakes Subsectional, which took in kids from eight states.

2. The *sectionals*—Eastern, Midwestern, and Western.

3. The *nationals,* which determine the national champions in each division and also decide who gets to represent the United States at—

4. The *worlds,* held usually in Europe or North America. Once you're good enough to make the "world team," as we call it, you don't have to compete in subsectionals or sectionals the next year. You go straight into nationals.

Then there are two other competitions "on the side," so to speak:

1. The *North Americans,* which were held every odd-numbered year right after nationals. They were started back during World War II to give American and Canadian skaters international competition. They've now been discontinued.

2. The *Winter Olympics,* held every four years, as everyone knows.

Though I was only eight, Miss Kohout pushed me up into the novice class against kids three and four years older "so you can reach junior level in another couple of years."

Our Wagon Wheel club was host to the subsectional that year. After figures, I was fourth; at last I would get to free-skate in competition.

My program went really well, I thought. However, no scores or placings were revealed until everyone had skated. Near the end of the evening, someone told me, "Janet, you'd better put your skates back on in case they call you out for a medal." I did.

Finally the awards were announced. "In third place for novice ladies . . ." not me.

"In second place . . ." again, not me. I turned and began walking toward the Wagon Wheel lobby.

I never did hear the first-place announcement. The next thing I knew some kids were grabbing me and yelling and pulling me back toward the rink. I was shocked!

The Midwestern sectionals in Denver in January included skaters from twenty-two states. I placed fifth in school figures,

27

but pulled up to second place overall. A few weeks later, my mom took me to the 1962 nationals in Boston so I could see what it was like. There were all new champions that year, since the entire U.S. team had been killed the year before in a plane crash on the way to the worlds in Prague. I was really impressed with all the beautiful skating, but I don't think I made a very good impression on at least some people as we left. We were at the Boston airport, and it seemed like a lot of the judges and skaters were there at the same time catching various flights.

I had gotten carsick on the way to the airport. My mom and I were sort of right in the middle of everyone and talking—when I proceeded to throw up all over the floor. It was terrible. Everyone just sort of stared at this little girl who for some reason was hanging around the country's best skaters.

Miss Kohout's idea about "a couple of years" before going into junior division turned out to be only one year. The next season, when I was nine, I was up against girls as old as seventeen in the subsectional at Rochester, Minnesota. Again, I shocked myself by winning. At the sectionals in Sioux City, I was third, which meant I got to go to the 1963 nationals in Long Beach. Once again I was the youngest entrant in a competition. At nationals, the younger skaters drop back one division, so I was in novice again.

When the school figures were completed, I was in eleventh place—dead last. We called grandpa that night and told him how I'd done so far. "It's really fun to be out here, even if I am in last place," I told him, laughing.

Grandpa is a little hard of hearing, and he thought I was crying, not laughing. He immediately began to console me, "That's all right, Janet, now don't feel bad. You'll do better tomorrow—"

"Grandpa, I'm *laughing!* We're having a great time!"

I did do better at free skating, managing to move up to tenth place overall. I also met Dick Button there, who was to become a close friend and adviser when I finally decided, ten years later, to turn professional.

The next summer, Miss Kohout took seventeen of us from the Wagon Wheel to an invitational, the Central Ontario

Free Skating Competition in Toronto. This was my first crack at the senior division (at age ten!) and also my first chance to see some of the very good Canadian skaters.

That winter, as a fifth-grader, I managed third in the senior division in the subsectional at Saint Paul. At Midwesterns in Detroit I landed a double axel cleanly—my first time in competition. I missed qualifying for nationals, though. My first place in free skating wasn't quite high enough to raise my fifth in figures.

By this time, I was starting to spend more and more weekends doing guest performances and exhibitions. This meant all the more work for my mother, who had to take care of all the correspondence getting sanctions for everything from the USFSA. In fact, we have seven or eight file drawers down in our basement full of the paperwork it took over the years to protect my amateur status. I know lots of people think amateurism is a bunch of hypocrisy, but I think it's very important. If you love sport enough, you'll do it without being paid. Now that I *am* being paid to skate, I'm glad that I learned to skate for the love of skating alone before the money came along.

There was really no way you could turn down an exhibition, even though it took a lot of time and didn't officially count for anything. It was just sort of an unwritten rule in skating that you went whenever asked. It showed that you cared about skating and giving people a chance to watch it. Naturally, you didn't knock yourself out trying the most difficult jumps or skating a full four minutes like in a competition, but there were always some people in the crowd who were knowledgeable and could tell if you're loafing. So in a sense you were still being judged.

I'd been passing the USFSA tests one by one, and finally whipped No. 8 at the end of summer skating school on August 29, 1964. I got a little gold medal, and the papers said I, being eleven, was the youngest girl ever to get one. It was hard for me to know what to do or how to act when honors like this would come. My most common response when someone complimented me at the rink was just to put my head down and say nothing. My mom was sure that people were offended; one time she got so upset she spanked me for it. But then she had second thoughts and decided that since I wasn't being rude, just shy, she should leave me like I was.

By this time, though, I was losing my shyness toward Miss Kohout. She was teaching me how to do harder and harder things, and when I couldn't do them right, both of us got pretty frustrated. She'd storm around the rink, "Why can't you do that? You've been trying it for an hour and you keep doing it wrong every time!"

And I'd come back, "I know it, I just can't do it!" and begin to cry.

A couple of times when I really got mad, she simply walked off my lesson. I definitely deserved that, I know, but it was because I was just trying too hard. She was trying to tell me that if I did not submit to her discipline as a coach, I would be wasting my time.

And I got the message. Every Saturday or Sunday night we had "workout," where all the kids were on the ice together for a group lesson. Miss Kohout always seemed to yell at me as much or more than anyone else during workout.

One night she said absolutely nothing. I didn't hear one criticism all evening.

It tore me up. I went home, locked myself in my room, and threw a tantrum. When my mom made me tell her what was wrong, I sobbed, "Miss Kohout doesn't like me anymore. She didn't yell at me all night!"

Yet she's more than just a coach. She worried about me—and all her other skaters—around the clock. Once she took me to dinner at the Wagon Wheel just to give me some pointers on table manners. She taught me how to be polite at competitions; she taught my parents all kinds of things about the skating world.

When I got into sixth grade, I had a really great teacher, Eleanora Anderson, who made it possible for me to get more ice time. I spent the entire morning at the rink, when the ice was clean for practicing figures, and went to school at one

*My proud grandpa and I the day I passed my gold figure test,
which qualified me for the senior division.*

o'clock. Miss Anderson would then stay *after* school for a full hour to help me with what had been covered during the morning. I was back at the Wagon Wheel by four-thirty and would stay until eight or so before going home to do homework.

That year at subsectionals in Green Bay, I took first— barely. The Midwesterns were back in Sioux City that year, and I came in second to Gail Newberry, who was from another very strong skating club, the Broadmoor in Colorado Springs. We both went to the 1965 nationals at Lake Placid, New York, where I placed eighth in junior ladies' division. One judge commented, "She just needs time."

My family has movies of most of my competitions starting from this point, and when I look at them, I can't believe I had so much energy back then! I was doing all these wild and daring things. I remember that 1964-65 program especially because one day, while Miss Kohout and I were working on the ending—a really fast step with the music "Strike Up the Band"—I couldn't do it and we both got frustrated and left the rink. Through my tears I said, "I'm never coming back!" and went on to school.

The next morning, naturally, I was back. But Miss Kohout wasn't. Someone else finally unlocked the rink for me. Miss Kohout never showed up the whole day.

She had been in a very serious accident the night before, had totaled her car, had cracked some ribs and gashed her head with glass really bad.

I appreciated her more from then on!

5
a rainy night
in berkeley

Miss Kohout, for all of her dedication to skating, knows a kid has to do a few other things in life. In planning my schedule each year (once school arrangements had been made), she always insisted that I take a day off each week so I wouldn't go stale at skating.

That day off was usually Monday. She encouraged me to fill it instead with things like ballet. I took lessons from Helen Olson in Rockford, who greatly affected my skating style. I also took organ lessons to get a better feel for moving to the music on the ice. For a long time my sister Carol and I went every Monday night to the Engstrom School of Dance in Oak Park, near Chicago, for ballet and gymnastics lessons. (Which was kind of weird—commuting back to Chicago from Rockford after the earlier years of doing the opposite!)

I moved into seventh grade at Lincoln Junior High School in the fall of 1965. They arranged my classes so I didn't have to show up till 10:15 A.M. I also started confirmation classes at church on Saturday mornings—which meant my mom driving me the fifteen miles to the rink early so I could skate a couple of hours before class, and then going back afterwards to skate some more.

My four-minute skating program was tougher than ever that year—five spins and sixteen jumps, including two double axels (you take off from the forward outside edge of one foot, do 2½ turns in the air, and land on the back outside edge of the other foot—Axel Paulsen of Sweden invented it). The big one was a triple salchow (a backward takeoff, three complete turns in the air, and a backward landing).

The competitions started off to be a repeat of the year before: first place in the subsectional at Minneapolis, then second to Gail Newberry again in the sectional at Colorado Springs on her home ice. Skating coaches can get a little eager sometimes. Someone came up to my dad there at the Broadmoor after figures and said, "Mr. Nowicki, I just think you ought to know that _ _ _ _ _ said to me this morning, 'How are we going to keep Janet out of nationals?' " My dad brushed it off as gossip.

But it did seem a little strange when at almost the last minute I found out I had to do my program the first thing when free skating began at eight o'clock in the morning. Skating first is bad luck on three counts: (1) you don't get a full warm-up, (2) you have to start right away while you're still out of breath (especially in the high Colorado altitude), and (3) judges tend to mark tougher at the beginning and ease up as they see what the competition is.

I was only twelve, and I didn't know whether there was anything tricky going on or not (I still don't)—I just went out and skated my best. I tried the triple salchow and missed the landing, but got back up off the ice and kept going, hardly missing a beat. I was mainly concentrating on form—the position of my hands, the angle of my free foot, all the stuff Miss Kohout and I had spent so many hours working on. When I finished, I was pleased with how I had skated.

34

I'm really glad that Miss Kohout protected me from the politics in skating. She knew what she had to do; she had learned how the game works and did what she could to keep me from getting hurt. She didn't like that side of competition, but she did it. And she shielded me from the constant psychological warfare as much as she could.

Now that I've turned pro, I wish I could go back and talk to all the ego-trippers in the amateur skating world. I'd just like to say, "Look, winning isn't everything. Someday it won't really matter all that much."

My hang-loose attitude was letting me have all kinds of fun; I remember during practice how Paul McGrath, one of the older skaters, would think up combinations (two or more jumps right in a row) for me to do. He'd come up with some absolute killers, like, "double axel/double axel/double loop"— and I'd go out on the ice and do them! I guess it never dawned on me to say, "Hey, you've got to be kidding."

My teachers at Lincoln let me take two weeks off to get ready for the 1966 nationals at Berkeley, California. (Those two weeks happened to include semester exams, which were nice to postpone!)

But all week long during practice in Berkeley, people were telling Miss Kohout, "Don't let her try the triple salchow. She'll be a lot better off doing a perfect program without it." Judges, even Dick Button, advised against it.

When the competition began, Gail and I dropped back again to the junior division and were one-two after figures. There were nine girls in the division, all at least fifteen years old except me. I was still taking things like white teddy bears with me on trips!

That Saturday night I was to free-skate, it was raining like crazy. Miss Kohout wasn't ready to leave, so I hopped a ride with somebody in a Volkswagen from the hotel to the rink. I got dressed, put my skates on, and went out to warm up. It seemed like most of the thirty-five hundred people there were prancing around looking for me, afraid I was going to be late. Miss Kohout finally got there, I think, just before I began. It was my first lesson in getting ready for competition all by myself.

I wasn't scared, only nervous (there's a difference); I just went out on the ice and did the best I could. When the time came, I went zipping into the triple—and landed it! (It's so funny in the movie: from that point on, I'm grinning from ear to ear.) I could have skated all night after that.

About a half-hour later, up in the press room, a sportswriter told me I'd just won the junior national championship. I couldn't believe it. I burst into tears. It was such a surprise, because I'd been in competition for so many years already and had never won a *sectional* title, let alone nationals.

Naturally, the press made a big deal out of little Janet Lynn, twelve years old, four-feet-six and eighty pounds, carrying home this big trophy. Even a judge, who must not have been watching too closely, stopped my dad in a hallway to say, "Nice triple axel your daughter did out there." (A triple axel is next to *impossible*—it's never been landed in competition.)

I went home to take my exams. I guess the break didn't hurt me any, because I still made the honor roll for the first semester. My family was proud of everything that had happened, but it wasn't like I was suddenly a superstar around home or anything. My brothers were doing well at football and wrestling at Guilford High School, and their walls in the family room (where we hang all the awards and stuff) were filling up as fast as mine. When reporters would say, "I bet your brothers are proud of you," I'd say, "Well, I'm proud of them, too," because I really was.

It was about this time that I began setting more definite goals for my skating. Miss Kohout makes all her students sit down at the beginning of the year and write out what they want to accomplish. I don't remember what I wrote for the different years, but I think in the back of her mind she had her own goal for me—to make that third slot on the 1968 Olympic squad. Peggy Fleming and Tina Noyes were almost sure to go.

Pint-sized champion.

William L. Udell

First trip to Europe—Easter 1966.

So her next idea was to take me to Europe over the 1966 Easter vacation to enter a competition at Oberstdorf, Germany, and generally to become known on the European skating scene. I'd never been away from home this long without my parents, and to top it off, my thirteenth birthday came while we were gone. I was terribly homesick; in fact, I cried nearly every night. But I came in second at Oberstdorf, and it seemed that everyone really liked my free skating.

We also spent some time at Davos, Switzerland, where we got to know George Hasler, the honorary secretary of the International Skating Union. Davos is actually two towns—

Davosdorf and Davosplatz. I was skating every day, of course. One day Miss Kohout and I went for a walk, looking in shops and just relaxing. I had to be back to the rink at a certain time to free-skate, but we weren't paying attention to the clock. We kept walking and walking, all the way through Davosplatz and almost to the other end of Davosdorf.

Suddenly we realized what time it was. We headed back. The faster Miss Kohout walked, the tireder I got and the more I dreaded having to go through my program once we got to the rink. Someone has said that it takes as much energy to do a four-minute free-skating program as it takes to play a whole game of football, and I believe it.

Miss Kohout kept trying to get me to walk faster and faster, and I kept trying to save my strength by slowing down.

Then, as if matters weren't bad enough, it started to snow. I started thinking about having to push all the harder on the snow-covered ice at that outdoor rink . . . eventually she was a full two blocks ahead of me while I trudged along feeling sorry for myself.

But we finally got to the rink, I still had to do my program, snow or no snow!

Back in Rockford, the further I went in junior high school, the more aware I became of what skating was costing me. I wanted so badly to be "in," to be a normal student with time for games and parties, and there just wasn't time. I still loved skating, but I began asking myself, "Why am I doing this?"

I wasn't a little kid anymore, out there popping off jumps and spins just because somebody told me to. I was searching for a better motivation. In my confirmation class, I found myself asking lots of questions about all sides of life: "Why are we living? Why are things in life so hard? What good is it to believe in a certain thing?"

Pastor Peterson is one of the world's more unusual ministers, and he had a good way of teaching the five sections of Martin Luther's *Small Catechism*. He said, "First, we discover we're sick—by using the Ten Commandments.

"Then, we look for a doctor." The Apostles' Creed was section two, which described God.

"We go to the Doctor." This is done through prayer, especially the Lord's Prayer.

"We accept His advice." This is what baptism is all about.

"And we go back for check-ups." This is done through the Lord's Supper, or communion.

Pastor says he could always tell by the look on my face when I didn't understand something. He saw that certain look quite a lot.

6
somebody new
inside

At the end of the school year, the confirmation class—
we seventh-graders as well as the eighth-graders—went up
to Camp Augustana near Lake Geneva, Wisconsin, for a week.
There must have been sixty or seventy of us altogether. It
was a neat time—a lot of softball, volleyball, swimming,
water skiing, and general messing around.

When we got there on Sunday afternoon, Pastor opened up
with a question-and-answer session so kids could ask anything that was on their minds. He let us know that he'd be staying in Cabin 1 all by himself, and that we were welcome to
stop by anytime we wanted just to talk and snack.

He didn't wait for kids to come to him, though. Before the
week was over, he'd been around to every cabin to serve us the
Lord's Supper and to talk about spiritual things.

Margie Sun and I had been close friends at church and were

together a lot. One afternoon, she and I and a counselor named Larry went out in a rowboat and headed across the lake. We started asking him many of our questions about Christ and salvation and our problems, and we got so involved that Margie and I ended up rowing all the way to the other side while he just loafed in the sun! But at least we got some of our questions answered.

Larry rowed on the way back, and we kept talking. It was good that no one else was around and we could come out with things that other kids didn't seem to be interested in.

Then one day Pastor passed out these little booklets called "The Four Spiritual Laws." He told us to memorize the four statements and the Scripture references that went with them.

So Margie and I did.

1. God loves you and has a wonderful plan for your life. *(John 3:16* and *10:10).*

2. Man is sinful and separated from God; thus he cannot know and experience God's love and plan for his life. *(Romans 3:23* and *6:23).*

3. Jesus Christ is God's only provision for man's sin. *(John 14:6).*

4. We must individually receive Jesus Christ as Savior and Lord. *(John 1:12, Ephesians 2:8,9,* and *Revelation 3:20).*

But we didn't really understand. The next night we went to Carol, our counselor, and said, "We memorized these like Pastor said, but we don't know what they mean."

She began explaining them to us and telling us how she had done what the fourth spiritual law said—she had invited Jesus Christ into her life on a personal basis. Now she knew her sins were forgiven and that God accepted her.

Margie and I still had a lot of questions. I said, "Why do I need to ask Jesus now? I've prayed all my life—at bedtimes, at competitions, you know." She explained that Christ had always been glad to hear my prayers, but that the real point was bigger than that—would I turn my life over to His control?

Lights were supposed to be out at midnight, but since we were with a counselor, we kept going. It was almost four in the morning before we resolved our questions. Then Carol asked us if we wanted to accept Christ right then. We both said yes. She told us we should ask for forgiveness and invite Christ to actually live inside of us.

So Margie prayed, and I prayed. It was a beautiful moment. I knew it was something that I wanted, that I even needed.

When we finished, we were crying because we were happy. I knew I didn't understand all about it and that I had a lot of learning and growing to do. But Carol said, "Remember, Janet, that Jesus is always with you, wanting to help you. When you feel afraid or inferior, give those feelings to Him. He promised to take them and give us peace.

"Don't forget, He can handle *anything*."

Later in the week, I said, "Carol, if Jesus is living inside me now, how come I don't feel any different?" I don't know what I was expecting—some emotional fly-away feeling or something.

She said, "Most of the time you won't. Actually, you don't need to. You took a step in faith—you believed what Jesus promised you and all of us in the Bible—and that's all you need. He won't let you down."

She was right.

I went through the second year of confirmation studies during eighth grade, and our class of forty-three was confirmed on May 14, 1967. I had missed some Saturdays, of course, because of skating, and my exhibitions were cutting out church on some Sundays as well. All of this meant that I didn't grow as fast as I should have after I became a Christian at camp.

I had to learn a lot of things on my own, just really searching my heart and asking God questions through prayers. And once in a while I'd suddenly see the light on something. I realized that I needed encouragement and help from other Christians, and at slumber parties sometimes Margie or I would start the conversation off on a spiritual track.

Sometimes all of us girls would even leave the house for a while and go over to church. I'd call Pastor at eleven-thirty or even later and say, "I'm sorry to bother you, but are you busy?"

He—already in bed or else hurrying to get there so he'd be ready for a big Sunday the next day—would say, "Oh, not really. Why?"

"Could you open up the church? A bunch of us want to

come over." We'd all go sit around on the floor in front of the altar, and he'd come over and sit with us and talk and answer questions for a couple of hours. Sometimes he'd serve the Lord's Supper.

Those were really beautiful times. About ten of my friends came to accept Christ over those years.

As a result, our church now has a "key club" of various laymen who can unlock the church throughout the week whenever people want to use it. And Gloria Dei has, even now, a service just for young people at ten-thirty every Saturday night.

It must have been in the Lord's plan that all the spiritual awakening came along at this time, because I really needed it. With all of my identity questions, my growth spurt (from four-feet-seven to five feet in less than a year), and traveling, I would have been in bad shape without the Lord to help me.

After winning subsectionals in Rockton and sectionals in Cleveland, I had to stay in the senior division at nationals, having won juniors the year before. The Rockford papers sent Sports Editor Rick Talley to Omaha to cover the story, and for the first season I was starting to feel pressure.

At Cleveland I had placed first in school figures—shock of my life!—but at Omaha, I wound up seventh. Naturally, I was hoping to pull that up to third with my free skating and thereby make the world team.

Well, I didn't. I pulled up to fourth. I can tell by looking at the movies that it was a confusing time for me. My positions weren't as finished; I tried two triple jumps and fell once.

But Miss Kohout and I went to the worlds in Vienna anyway, just as I had gone to nationals back in 1962 before I actually got to compete. I was officially the first alternate for the U.S. team, and I learned a lot just by watching.

That August I was back in Europe for a two-week exhibition tour with Peggy Fleming and some others. Miss Kohout had spent a lot of time helping perfect my program for the tour. I was excited and nervous, but skated about the best I ever have. European skaters are usually very well-disciplined at school figures but not always as flashy at free skating. I remember some tour people getting a little tight about all the applause this young fourteen-year-old was getting!

But I was starting to realize that the reason I could skate well was that the Lord was helping me. My family was doing its share and more as well. Before I left on that trip, my brother Glenn took the lawn mowing money he'd been saving for a bike and bought me a raincoat. It was like that all the time at our house. Skating kept us very humble and very close together, because there never was enough money to buy everything everyone wanted. We each had to give up a few things for the other.

7
grenoble

It was getting to be Olympic time. We speeded up my first semester of ninth grade. I took a programmed learning course in math and made some other changes so that I was all done by Christmas.

After subsectionals and sectionals, we went to the nationals in Philadelphia January 18-21. Rick Talley was along again, and he wrote a column that describes the figures competition pretty well:

> It was cold, damp and very, very dark here Friday morning when Janet Lynn walked down the steps of the not-so-glittering Belvue-Stratford Hotel.
>
> Her breakfast was finished. She had awakened at 5 a.m. and had eaten cold steak and orange juice in her 14th-floor room.
>
> By 6:30 a.m. she was at the Spectrum, an athletic monstrosity which houses Philadelphia's pro hockey and basketball

46

teams . . . a cold, gray concrete oval with dangerously narrow corridors and hidden locker rooms . . . .

Skating began at 7 a.m.

This was her bid for the United States Olympic team . . . .

It was not an easy morning for a 14-year-old . . . for a little, blue-eyed blonde who stands just a fraction over five feet tall and barely weighs 100 pounds.

It was quiet on the ice.

Nine onlookers—five official judges, three standbys and a referee—stood ominously in their crepe-soled boots, bulky overcoats and stocking caps, clutching clipboards with flapping pages in their gloved hands.

Overhead, pigeons flew softly through the Spectrum's girders.

Janet had to be a little nervous. Her face was as white as her white wool dress, a soft, supple 49-button garment made by her mother.

"I haven't been able to talk to her much for two days," admitted her father. "She's concentrating . . . ."

Now there was activity. An occasional shush of blade on ice . . . and later, as more spectators arrived, some scattered applause.

Skating the compulsory figures for judges is a lonely experience . . . there is no music, as in free skating, and there's no one beside the skater to offer counsel.

The worst, however, is the waiting.

After each of her figures, Janet would walk up the concrete stairs, slip into her overcoat and sit silently with her mother and Miss Kohout, while others performed.

Occasionally, she'd sip through a straw from a milk protein mixture prepared by her father, manager of Lenz Pharmacy in Rockford. It's a quick-energy formula.

Then she'd slip off her skates to rest her feet . . . and Mrs. Nowicki would thrust her hands into them to keep the leather from getting cold.

Mr. Nowicki, not trusting the elaborate computer system installed to tabulate quick results, spent his time roaming the halls and corridors, copying down judges' reports and analyzing Janet's standing.

Later, when the computer system suffered a breakdown, he was the only person on top of the scoring—and he quipped to Slavka, "You should know you can't replace me with a computer."

47

. . . During the morning, Janet walked up and down the two-story, concrete stairs at least 24 times. No waiting room had been provided for skaters . . . so they always returned to wait with their instructors, or families, for the results of each figure.

When it was over . . . when the last pencil mark had gone onto the scoresheet and the last ice mark was erased . . . Janet relaxed.

She had finished fourth in a field of 12 . . . and she knew she still had a good chance to become one of the youngest Olympic team members in United States history . . . .

That's about how it went, not only at Philadelphia but at most competitions.

I about died when all of a sudden my brother Glenn showed up! Larry was already a freshman at the Air Force Academy by then, but Glenn was a senior at Guilford. He and four other guys left after school on Friday and drove *eight hundred fifty miles* to see me skate four minutes on Saturday evening. I couldn't believe it. (Glenn kept making those surprise appearances in years to come, too; he always got a big kick out of shocking me.)

My free-skating program used Debussy's "Afternoon of a Fawn," which was a little discordant for the straight-laced world of figure skating. But the judges didn't seem to object. My skating seemed to be getting more meaning and expression.

But when I did it that night, I fell on the triple salchow and again on the double lutz. Judges are supposed to ignore falls and judge only what you are able to complete, but there's hardly a way for them to totally forget it when you fall.

Dick Button was doing ABC's commentary that night, and we have it in our movies. It's so funny—he's raving on and on about "little Janet Lynn—only needs to move up one place to make the Olympic team—she's moving gracefully, powerfully—isn't she fantastic!—a beautiful jump!" and on and on.

Then I fall for the second time, and Dick goes: "Oh! I don't know what's happening to her tonight!"

Anyway, I moved into third. The United States would be

represented in figure skating at the Tenth Winter Olympics by Peggy Fleming, nineteen years old, five-time national champion; Tina Noyes, twenty years old, from New York City; and me.

Before leaving Philadelphia, I had an interview with a minister who wanted to write a magazine article about me. Rick Talley happened to be in the room and heard us talking about church, my accepting Christ a year and a half before, and my faith.

Rick went back to Rockford and began working on a series of newspaper articles. The day the Olympics opened in France —February 6—his article in the *Register-Republic* had this headline: "Janet Lynn's Philosophy: God Has Plan for Her to Skate." It started out sounding almost like the Four Spiritual Laws.

> Janet Lynn has a philosophy.
> She believes that everybody is good for something . . . and that God has a plan for everyone's life.
> She believes that a person's goal should be to find what God's plan is for his life . . . then do his best to fulfill that plan.

A lot of people in Rockford were shocked. Even I was kind of taken by surprise when I heard about it, but it was fine. After all, there wasn't any reason to hide something so important in my life from sportswriters.

The article went on to talk about my faith in God (even when I fell in Philadelphia) and my church background; it also had quotes from Pastor Peterson.

From that time on it was easier for me to talk openly about my inner feelings and my relationship to the Lord. Naturally, I started getting invitations to speak for church groups, which scared me to death. My mom urged me to go ahead and try, and this helped me overcome some more of my shyness.

In Grenoble, I really felt lost among all the big names of the skating and skiing world. I spent a lot of time in my room alone. Then one day in the elevator a skater my age named

49

*The 1968
Winter
Olympics in
Grenoble,
France:
Tina Noyes,
Peggy Fleming,
and me.
Below:
Grandpa,
Glenn, and
dad watching
me on TV
during the
wrestling
meet.*

Rockford Newspapers, Inc.

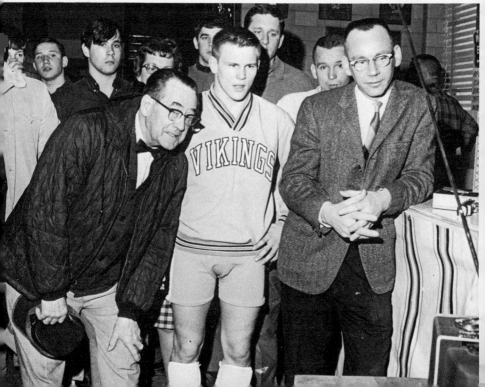

In Geneva, Miss Kohout tries to get her sickly skater going.

Hyun Joo Lee from Korea spoke to me. It felt great, even though we couldn't speak each other's language.

By the time the Olympic Games opened, I had a serious case of the flu. It had been coming on all week while we were practicing, and mom had been giving me medication. But then she had to stop just as I was getting better for fear that I might be one of the athletes chosen for a drug test and would be disqualified.

The doctor told me not to march in the opening ceremonies that first day. But there was *no way* I was going to miss that experience. It was one of the truly thrilling times of my life to march into that arena behind the flag of my country. There's something about your country and your flag that means so much more when you're in somebody else's country.

Even if I hadn't been sick, I would still have had everything I could do to find my way around, get to the rink at the right times, and be ready to perform. Most of the Grenoble cab drivers had been brought in from out of town and didn't know the area. So I soon learned the French words for "left" and "right."

Rick Talley called from Rockford one day. Miss Kohout said I was doing pretty well, but that I missed good old American hamburgers. Before I knew it, McDonald's had heard about it and had put thirty pounds of hamburger, buns, catsup, mustard, and pickles—enough for all 119 members of the American team!—on an Air France jet headed for Grenoble.

There were thirty-two figure skaters competing, and after compulsories I stood fourteenth. (You only had to do five figures in the '68 Olympics instead of six.) The pills approved by the Olympic officials didn't help me at all—in fact, they made me sicker. The day I free-skated, though, I felt better, and I wasn't any more nervous than usual. I did the same program as at Philadelphia, but without falling this time, and it had more feeling to it, more softness. It won sixth place, which, added with my school figures, came to ninth place overall.

Peggy, of course, won the gold medal, and we were all excited about that. There were two other girls above me whom I would get to know in future competitions: tall Beatrix (Trixi)

Schuba of Austria in fifth and Karen Magnussen of Canada in seventh.

There was considerably more excitement in Rockford, I guess, with everyone watching on TV. Glenn had a conference wrestling match at Guilford right at the time I was skating, so my dad rigged up a TV set at school so he could watch both his kids at once.

(Glenn lost his title match that day—too much thinking about me, I guess. But he learned his lesson. One of the next times I was on TV from Europe, he was again scheduled to wrestle. He charged onto the mat, pinned the poor guy in about thirty seconds, and came running to watch me!)

We left Grenoble for Geneva, Switzerland, where the world championships in figure skating were to begin about a week after the Olympics finished. Before we left the hotel, my Korean friend came to my room to say good-by. She gave me a handkerchief and a note that said, "Your friend, Joo Lee."

(I ran into her almost four years later, after I'd finished high school and was skating at the Broadmoor getting ready for another Olympics. We still write to each other.)

By the time we reached Geneva, my flu had turned into strep throat. My mom was going out of her mind caring for me and being unable to use the medicine my dad had sent along. One night my fever got up to 105 and I became delirious. I was thrashing around and talking nonsense.

Mom picked up the phone and called dad (our phone bill that month must have been unbelievable). "What do I do? She's out of her head, and I can't give her anything for fear she'll be thrown out of worlds."

My dad said, "If she's that sick, give her the pills and sacrifice the competition if you have to."

I don't know how I ever made it through figures. I could hardly breathe or swallow. I'd go down on the ice, do one, come back up, and lie on a bench shivering in my coat until time to do the next one. My free skating went pretty good, though, and I wound up once again in ninth place.

The best part of the whole seven-week trip, actually, was the last couple of days. We went back to Davos just to relax before coming home. I skated an exhibition, but most of the time I spent learning to ski, which was really fun.

We flew home from Zurich on Saturday, March 9, and when we got to O'Hare Field in Chicago, the airplane owned by the Rockford newspapers was there with my family to take us the rest of the way. It was so great to see my family again—we got a great chance to catch up on everything.

Then we landed in Rockford around six o'clock and I took one look out the window . . . there must have been a thousand people out there with signs and everything! I said, "Oh, no—I think I'll sleep in the plane tonight." It was wild. The mayor was there to proclaim Janet Lynn Day, and there was a motorcade downtown with me riding on the city's new twenty-eight-thousand-dollar fire truck! I was tired but happy, and just kind of overwhelmed by it all.

When I got home, the celebration continued. A bunch of kids from school were there and had decorated the house with signs and streamers.

And then suddenly, the Olympic bubble was gone. I didn't skate for a week. The next Monday morning, March 11, I walked back into Lincoln Junior High School for the first time since Christmas and started catching up.

8
trying to be just me

Every summer that came along found me fighting a bigger and bigger war with my weight. By the time I got out of junior high I had grown as tall as I was going to—5'1½"—and my whole body chemistry had changed from the T-bone-steak-every-night routine when I was a little girl.

Everybody in my family likes to eat. My brothers were always stashing it away, and I was in sports just like them, and I thought I could keep up with them at the table. It got to be an obsession in my mind: "I have to eat, I'm skating so much, I really need this food."

At times my weight would get up as high as 119 or 120, and then I couldn't skate or do anything right. Miss Kohout would tell me when I looked heavy, but wouldn't really nag me about it. She'd just tell my mom so *she* could get mad at me.

I knew that every year before competitions I'd have to get

down to around 108. And somehow I did, often by using the Weight Watchers plan. But then I'd go back up again, and to this day I'm still doing too much up-and-down-and-up-again.

Skating is good for your body because it develops coordination and balance—but it also develops some other things: beefy leg muscles and a big fanny. That was part of the price I especially resented once I entered high school in the fall of 1968.

Skating made high school hard in other ways as well. I never had time for things like pep club; in fact, I did good to fit in all the courses I needed. When I was younger, I had been a really good student, but now it seemed like I was always cramming. I hated not being prepared for class discussions . . . flunking pop quizzes . . . having to fake it on essay tests.

In fact, that was one of my biggest frustrations: faking it. I'd come to school at 11:15 after three or four hours of skating, and maybe I'd be down about something . . . and I'd walk the halls between classes and see the same kids every day and say "Hi!" every time . . . and there was nothing new to talk about.

I kept wondering, "How can I be real today? How can I say 'Hi' because I mean it, not just because they're standing there?"

The popular kids always seemed to be having a big time, playing jokes on each other and yukking it up . . . and yet to me it seemed all on the surface. Most kids didn't understand my frustrations, and I couldn't expect them to. Everyone seemed out just to impress.

I'd always had a few close friends, girls in the neighborhood who understood me and had been my friends before I got good at skating. Yet even with them, I felt like I didn't fit sometimes . . . like I had to be more disciplined, more adult, had to learn faster and get along with more diverse kinds of people, all because of who I was. And most of the time I didn't want to be different. I wanted to be ordinary Janet Nowicki.

Margie and I would see each other in the hall and say, "I feel 'dead.' " The word had a special meaning for us—like we were not even there, we were just walking along in the swirl disconnected from everybody, from God, even from ourselves. It was like a vacuum.

Yet there were some good times, too, that proved to me that I was a human being after all and not some skating weirdo. Times when Mom would take a whole bunch of us to a football game, and we'd goof around and act stupid (and never see the game!). Times at slumber parties when we'd go hopping inside our sleeping bags across the street to a playground at three o'clock in the morning.

When Glenn left for the University of Missouri, I moved downstairs to his room so I could be alone more. One night some of my girlfriends came over, and it got late enough that I should have gone to bed, since I had to skate the next morning. (That was the story of my life.)

But I didn't feel like sleeping. I hadn't been out at night for a long time. We decided we wanted to go out and drive around and see some kids. The problem was: How am I going to get out of the house?

I already had my pajamas on, so we decided I'd have to pretend to be going to bed and then crawl out the window. We went downstairs, where my grandpa was playing his usual game of solitaire. I said good-by to the girls and they left.

They came around to my bedroom window and whispered, "Come on, Tenaj!" (that was my nickname—*Janet* spelled backwards. They did the same thing to *Nowicki* and called me Icki-won.) But I couldn't make it out the window. So then I said, "Well, grandpa is hard of hearing, so I guess I'll try to sneak behind him and out the door!"

I put on my robe and went quietly tiptoeing along. I had to go right behind his back . . . I opened the door ever so silently and stepped outside—he never heard a sound!

We all laughed and thought we were cool as we went driving around (I don't know why—I was the one who would suffer the next day on the ice). Some kids we went to see were asleep already, so we banged on their windows.

Finally, I realized I had another problem: How am I going to get back in? I said, "Well, I'll just have to try the same way I got out!" I went back to the downstairs door—and the light was still on. Grandpa was *still* playing solitaire. So again I went silently through the door . . . past him . . . and on into my bedroom—and again he didn't see or hear me!

But then at other times I felt distant from even these friends. I was out of school for around nine weeks every winter, and when I'd get back from Europe I'd have so much to talk about that nobody else was interested in. I had learned so much traveling and being with kids from all over, and I'd want to share it, and all my friends seemed totally wrapped up in Rockford. Even Margie and I didn't talk for almost a year at one point.

And I wanted to say, "Hey, you guys, you have to *search* a little bit in life!" People are always wondering where they can find meaning or find God when they haven't turned themselves inside out. If you really search and evaluate your real motives—*even if it hurts*—you will find Him. Most people won't leave their warm little existence to do any digging.

I guess that's what Jesus meant when He said if you try to save your life, you will lose it.

That first fall at Guilford more or less set the pattern of three courses per semester plus an independent study course. Carl Nielsen, my guidance counselor, did a lot of planning to get my courses clustered into one part of the day so I could skate the rest, and then to get my teachers to figure out things I could do to keep up while traveling.

I always took September off from skating (so I could get a good jump on school) and May as well (to finish up in the spring). That fall I was doing a University of Nebraska extension course in geometry along with my three regular classes, and Mr. Nielsen could see that I wasn't going to get done by the first of December, when I needed to start skating full-time. So he arranged for a tutor.

He went to one math teacher and said, "I have a sophomore who needs some tutoring in geometry. Would you like to take this on? You'd make six dollars an hour."

She sort of sighed and said, "Oh, I don't have the time."

Mr. Nielsen said, "Fine," and went on to offer the job to another math teacher. She said, "Yeah, I guess I can fit it in."

Then he said, "Okay, the student is Janet Lynn." We worked together and I got done with the course in time.

But I guess when the first teacher found out who she had turned down, she went storming into Mr. Nielsen's office: "Why didn't you say it was Janet Lynn?!"

"That didn't have anything to do with it," he told her. "I only wanted to know whether you wanted to help a kid with geometry." She was mad at him for months.

But I really appreciated him trying to keep me from being a big name. He never hand-picked my teachers or courses— in fact, I was registered by computer like everyone else. And he says that none of my teachers ever complained about letting me work faster and quit early (or start late). It was the teachers I *didn't* have who sometimes came around and said, "How come we're making things so slick for Janet?" And then he'd say, "No we're not. Here's what she's doing . . . ."

When I got to nationals in Seattle in January 1969, it was the first time I'd competed in ten months. Peggy Fleming had turned pro, and Tina, after placing second to Peggy at four nationals in a row, was hoping this was finally her year. In fact, it was now or never, since she was already twenty-one.

There was a new scoring rule for which I was very grateful: figures and free skating were now counted on a 50-50 basis instead of 60-40. Even so, you can't really say the two were equal, because judges always mark figures tougher than they do free skating. A mediocre figure will get you somewhere around 3.5 (6.0 is perfect). A mediocre free-skating program usually gets around 5.2 to 5.5. In other words, there's still more to lose on figures.

Like the year before in Philadelphia, I was fourth after figures. This was the first year I hadn't had to go through subsectionals and sectionals, and I could tell it. My free-skating program ran out of steam a little at the end, but the triple went perfect.

When the points were totaled there was only .59 between

Judges in Seattle scrutinizing my school figures in 1969, the year I became national champion. The Seattle Tin

the top three places. Tina was third. Julie Holmes, another Broadmoor skater, was second. And I was the national ladies' champion.

I know it was an absolute heartbreak for Tina. She told a reporter, "Halfway through (the free-skating routine), I started to get tight. I knew I had to relax, but my legs felt

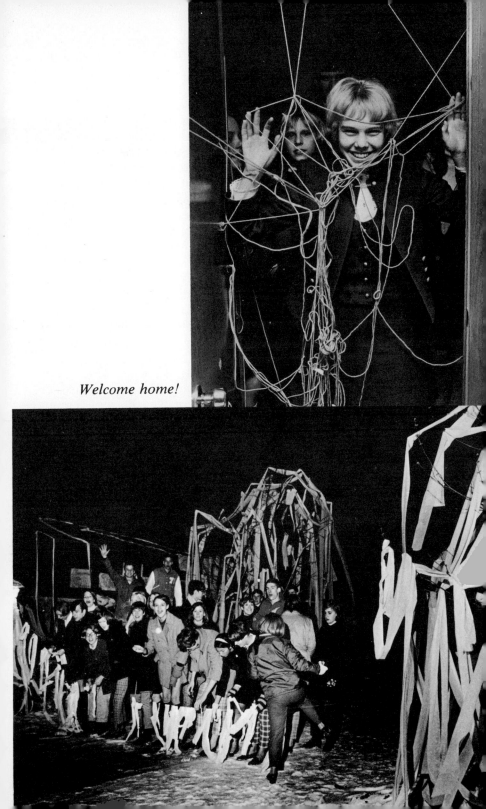

Welcome home!

stiff. The music would fade inside of me. I was blowing it, and I couldn't do anything about it . . . Skating has been everything for seven years. Oh, why did I let this get away?"

The North American championships were to be held in Oakland the next week. Karen Magnussen had just gone through a defeat, too, as Linda Carbonetto had taken away her Canadian title. That made Karen all the tougher—she's the kind of person who can really bear down when she wants to win something.

Karen led slightly after compulsories, and the rest of us were pretty close. Her free-skating program on Saturday night was really good. I was the last to skate, and after it was over, Karen and I were together waiting for the results to be announced. I was pretty sure she would still be on top, and so I said, "Congratulations."

She bit her lip and said, "Not yet."

When the announcement came, it was even closer than at Seattle: Janet Lynn, 2,215.5 points; Karen Magnussen, 2,214.1 points. All of a sudden there was Peggy Fleming handing me this big silver bowl.

I don't think I could have stood another close one like that. It was good to get on the plane the next day and go home. This time Mayor Schleicher of Rockford and a lot of other important people had driven in to O'Hare to meet me. And when I got home, about forty Guilford kids had used *eighty* rolls of toilet paper on my house, trees, bushes, and everything! The doorway to my room was a maze of string like a spider's web; I couldn't even get in.

The next morning, they even came back to clean up the mess while I slept!

I spent the next couple of weeks getting ready for worlds, which were held at the Broadmoor in Colorado Springs. It was a good chance to visit Larry at the Air Force Academy. He got to come see me skate—after going through all kinds of military red tape in order to stay out late. Then the competition fell behind schedule, and he almost missed his curfew.

It turned out to be a strange competition: Karen suddenly had to drop out because of *vertical* leg fractures, possibly from overpractice. Hana Moskova, the Olympic bronze medal-

ist from Czechoslovakia, hurt her back and had to quit as well.

I was nervous and tight during the figures—suddenly here I was, a punk fifteen-year-old supposed to be national and North American champion, up against all these fantastic skaters from Europe. Dick Button teased me and tried to get me to relax, but after I left he commented, "The knife is twisting in her stomach. You can see it in her eyes."

Well, the world title went to Gabriele Seyfert of East Germany. I ended up fifth behind Julie Holmes in fourth. I was disappointed with myself, because I knew I could have skated better.

Every year after worlds, the top skaters do an exhibition tour. It's really neat, because you can relax and just enjoy skating and traveling. You don't often get close to anybody during competitions, because everyone is concentrating in her own little shell, and there's a tension between you as competitors even if you don't want it to be there.

But on tour, it's different. We did four weeks of one-night shows all over the United States and Canada. It was another rare chance to be real with people.

9

"better than"

I've probably already gone further in this book than I should have without explaining how I feel about competing.

I skate because I love to skate and want to try to radiate love to the people. I don't skate to beat anybody. At least most of the time. I've had just enough times when I slipped into the cutthroat attitude—"I am out here to win, I don't care whether the crowd enjoys it or not, just so I win"—to know that I don't like it.

Competition can bring out some terribly negative feelings. I'm so glad to be a professional now with the Ice Follies where I can just skate and not have to worry about the other girl. When I first went with the show I mentioned that I wasn't a competitor. Some people said, "Oh, yes you were! In all those championship contests you were a great fighter."

But that's not true. In fact, whenever I went on the ice with the feeling, "I want to be *better than* Karen" (or Trixi or Julie or whoever), I didn't communicate the love through skating that I wanted to. And it showed up even in the technical aspects.

I've been told that this philosophy is really radical in the sports world . . . that Vince Lombardi would turn over in his grave to hear me talk like this. But I can't identify with his slogans, like "Winning isn't everything—it's the only thing" and "The only substitute for victory is disgust." There were lots of times when I came off the ice without winning that I wasn't disgusted. It would have been wrong to be disgusted. I had skated well and had given something to the audience, and that, to me, was the point of it all.

Most people don't understand; they say, "You can't have that attitude when you're in competition." Some are downright cynical: "Come on, Janet, you know you wanted to come home from Sapporo with that gold medal. . . ." Yes, I did, but not so I could say I was a better skater than every other girl in the world. I wanted it only because it would have been a symbol of excellence, and it would have given me a lot of chances to tell how Christ has helped me. As a matter of fact, I got those chances anyway, so I didn't really lose anything.

Don't get me wrong: I believe in setting goals. Miss Kohout made us do it every year, and I've set a lot of goals on my own. That's the only way to bring the best out of yourself. But you can't make that your whole life and call yourself worthless if you don't reach your goal. There's a subtle difference between striving for excellence as a way of interacting with God and with your audience—and gritting your teeth in vengeance to be "better than."

I have learned over the years that hatred is wrong for me. I'm not perfect in this area, but I want to be. Otherwise, I just get into a lot of tension and pressure that shouldn't be there. I can't be friends with the other skater, I can't be honest, I get jealous if she wins, and all kinds of ugly things happen when I start trying to beat.

And besides all that, I skate worse. It doesn't bring out

my best skating—just the opposite. I've proved that over and over.

Maybe, if I'd started thinking the other way when I was young, I could have made myself want to win so badly I could have done it. But I wouldn't have been genuine in my smiling and everything; it would all have been just an act to impress the judges. That's not what the Lord wanted.

When I was little I guess I was taken up with the challenge of learning all about skating. But soon I started really loving the freedom of being on the ice. I'd be practicing, and some music would be playing, and I would just start skating to the music. And soon I'd be lost in myself, moving along, not caring what I looked like or anything, just doing what I felt on the inside and being creative.

That's why school figures never appealed to me—I couldn't see anything creative in them. They were just something you *had* to do, the more rigid, the better.

As I got older, I had to face the question: If I am not out here to be competitive, what am I here for? Why? That's when I started turning more toward the Lord and asking Him to take my skating and use it as an expression of love. And every once in a while I'll notice sentences in the fan mail like, "There's something unusual about your skating" or "Your skating is so refreshing" or "When I watch you skate, there's something spiritual about it." I intend it to be more than just artistic; I ask the Lord before I go on the ice to help me to love every minute, every move I make, and to pour love out to the crowd. I don't always succeed, because it's tiring emotionally. But that's my goal.

Miss Kohout's last words before her students go on the ice are usually, "Go out there and tell a story." She doesn't fall apart if you lose. She's a perfectionist. She's always said, "Skate well, and that's the best you can do. No one can ask you to do better. If they judge you unfairly or whatever, it doesn't matter, just so long as you skate well."

Some people have said, "Then how do you get psyched up for a competition? If the point is not to win, what's the difference between a competition and an exhibition—or even an ordinary practice?"

The difference is in the audience. A competition audi-

"Go out there and tell a story!"

ence is usually bigger—sometimes you're on television as well—and they know more about skating than an ordinary crowd. So you want to show them the best you can do. In your own mind you've set up this competition as a goal, a place for measuring your progress. And you have to be ready to "tell your story" the very best you can at *one certain time,* and you won't get another chance for a full year.

You start building seriously toward that moment at least a couple of months before, when you put together your program. I remember about three weeks before competitions I'd reach a plateau where I was skating all right, but not good enough. It was the only time of the year when I got genuinely *scared.* I had to *push* myself further or else just sit on the plateau, which meant eventually sliding down.

I'd go into half a week of crying, worrying, fearing, and agonizing. I'd pray, "Lord, I know I have to get further than this, and I know that You'll help me." I'd start really pushing myself, and soon I could tell that I was off the plateau and climbing again.

It got so each year I could tell when I was stuck on the plateau, and I'd go, "Oh, no! Not this point again." And then the Lord would have to help me fight off the desire just to rest.

Then I really had to do a lot of praying the day of competition to keep from giving in to worry and tension. I'd hear myself saying, "Well, I feel pretty good now, but how am I going to feel tonight? I've got another eight hours to go. . . ." And I would just have to pray, "Lord, I don't need to feel good now; I'm not doing anything now. I'll be emotionally worn out if I keep this up all afternoon. I'm just going to forget about it, and You make sure I have the right feelings at the right time."

The pressure seemed to keep coming at me in waves all day. I'd find myself seesawing back and forth: *I've just got to skate well tonight—Lord, take it! . . . I've got to skate well tonight—Lord, take it!*

And He would.

10
bearing down

In April of my sophomore year I turned sixteen, which meant I could finally drive myself back and forth to the rink, to school, to Chicago for gymnastics lessons, and everywhere. What a relief for my mother!

Driving time became thinking time for me. Time to sort through my feelings, to figure out answers to questions, to brood, to ask God why on all sorts of things.

I fought lots of hours against my parents' discipline and the whole rigid system of training I was in. Both my folks and Miss Kohout are disciplinarians; my dad still tells about sitting down with my mom back in the fifties and discussing the psychologists' new idea for raising kids: permissiveness. (Not long ago in Japan, he got mixed up and kept saying "submissiveness," which, after translation, had everyone thoroughly confused!)

They, to put it bluntly, decided against it. Their kids were not going to be allowed to do anything that popped into their adventurous minds.

And so my folks were really strict—I thought. We had to be in by midnight (if I wasn't, they'd call the parents of the guy I was with.) If we went out one night, we couldn't go out the next. If we didn't have our homework done, we couldn't go out. If they felt like we were just having parties all the time and weren't doing anything constructive, they'd say so. If we weren't doing our work around the house, we'd hear about it.

I did my share of rebelling by the way I acted toward them, or their friends. One time I sort of unloaded on Glenn in a letter. Here's part of it:

> Man, do I wish you were home. There are so many things I want to talk to you about, but the most prevalent one is about how I feel.
>
> When I got home I was *so* happy to see *everyone*. You wouldn't believe how I felt . . . I even felt like working around the house! It only lasted a couple of days, though. It's slowly wearing off. Now, it is like coming back into reality with all life's problems. On tour we didn't have to worry about anything 'cause the officials would worry about transportation and everything. I guess I got used to not having to worry. Believe it or not—mom didn't pick on me hardly at all and we had a great time. As soon as I got home she started being herself again. The first night I said maybe I was just tired. It's still not much better.

From there I went on to talk about a guy I'd been dating who didn't seem to be sure whether he liked me now or not, and a bunch of other stuff. Typical high-school hassles, I guess.

But sometimes driving along, I got to the place where I felt like I did nothing right. My folks told me so many things I was doing wrong, and I would think about it, and after a while I'd say to myself, "Unfortunately, they're right again!" I never admitted that to them, of course.

At times I felt so much like nothing. I had been trying, but my trying wasn't good enough for them or anyone. I thought about running from it all, just running away. One time I even thought, "It sure would be easy to just swerve over in front of that other car and commit suicide. Then I wouldn't have to submit to all this discipline anymore." But then I thought I'd probably kill somebody else at the same time, and that wouldn't be right.

It took a long time for the Lord to convince me that He uses parents to punish us. I just despised them sometimes; I wanted to say, "Go away, leave me alone." But the Lord kept me from doing anything drastic while I learned more about submitting to authority. And I found that if I would submit to my parents and obey them, I could submit to God and obey Him more easily.

Sometimes when I'd get to the rink, I'd be feeling just terrible. I couldn't skate or jump or do anything right. Miss Kohout would say, "Come on, tell me what's wrong. Do you want to talk about it?" We'd spend almost my whole lesson talking.

Then, during the last five minutes, when I was exhausted from crying, we'd try to accomplish at least one thing on the ice!

Other times, she would know that I simply *had* to go through my four-minute program that day, and she'd say, "All right, cut the crying and go do your number." She'd push me through it even though I was sobbing every step, because she knew I had to do it to reach my peak by competition time.

I'll never forget one morning in Colorado Springs when I was a junior. It was a couple of weeks before I had to defend my title in Tulsa at nationals, and she had decided to take six of us to do our training in the high altitude. I did my program, and then Miss Kohout started bearing down on the fast part with most of the difficult jumps. She made me keep doing it over and over again, with no rest in between, and I could see she wasn't going to give up until it was right.

Finally, on about the sixth time, I fell on the double axel. I tightened up as I hit the ice, and my ankle sprained. I went hobbling off.

"Where are you going?" she yelled.

I said, "I did something to my ankle."

She thought I was faking. "Get back out here and do it right this time."

I said, "Miss Kohout, I *can't*. My ankle's hurt."

I spent the next few days with my foot in the whirlpool, talking to Tim Wood, the national men's champion who had also sprained his ankle. The trainer from the Air Force Academy was there and gave us massages and taped us up.

But I got no sympathy whatever from Miss Kohout. I think she felt badly, but she knew what I had to accomplish yet. In fact, she wouldn't even talk to me until I got back on the ice four days later.

The truth is, though, that my skating at Tulsa was among the best I ever did. Both Tim and I kept our titles.

The worlds in 1970 were in Ljubljana, Yugoslavia. We stopped to train in Switzerland, and Miss Kohout hadn't changed a bit. The rink was outdoors this time, and it snowed every day. Every morning she and mom would be out there shoveling up to a foot of snow off the rink themselves. They worked as hard as I did. Mom would have to keep shoveling patches throughout the day while I spent five to six hours on figures.

When it came to practicing my program, there was simply no way to shovel the entire rink. So I just had to go plowing through the drifts. She'd keep making me do it, skating right behind me until, out of sheer desperation, I landed every jump.

Then came her clincher: "See, you *can* do everything right, no matter how tired you are or how bad the conditions."

When we got to Ljubljana, I didn't do everything right; I placed sixth, one slot lower than the year before. Though my free skating became much stronger, my figures got much worse. The tour wasn't quite as much fun, either, because so much of it was through communist countries. The

73

Soviet Union was just super-depressing to me. You'd ask for some ice cream at the end of a meal in the hotel, and the waiter would say, "We'll see." You never got your ice cream.

The more I saw of Russian skaters, the more I saw the effects of their system. Some of them are very good, especially in pair skating, and there was always a lot of talk about whether their training can be called amateur. Because it's true that if a Russian kid shows some talent at skating, he's offered government training—and that's all he does from then on. He doesn't get a salary, but the government sports committee pays every expense you can think of.

I don't really object to that; they have a different way of running their country, and that's okay. What bothered me was the lack of heart and feeling in so many Russian skaters. Some of them seemed just like machines. Machines never make a mistake, it's true—but they don't communicate anything to you, either.

So maybe there's something to be said for getting entirely away from skating some of the time. I could never talk about skating, for example, with a guy I was dating. I didn't want to, and neither did he.

Yet we couldn't avoid it sometimes. The most embarrassing part of any date was to be in Rockford and to have to stop and sign an autograph. We'd be walking down a street and hear kids say, "Hey, there's Janet Lynn!"

I started double-dating when I was in ninth grade, and began dating alone the next year, even though my folks had wanted me to wait until I was a senior. I dated about four guys seriously throughout high school, and I'm still friends with all of them now. But I'd say it was hard for me to be myself, to be completely honest a lot of the time.

It was hard to control physical desires, which can really confuse the issue if you get carried away and don't seek the Lord's help. He helped with this kind of discipline—if I was willing to "die to myself," so to speak, and not disgrace Him by what I wanted.

While I was in summer school (as always, trying to collect enough credits to graduate on time), a guy I dated spent the summer working at a camp run by Young Life,

74

which is a Christian club for high-school kids. We used to go to the weekly meetings throughout the school year, too. At the end of the summer, he had the whole work crew at his house for a weekend. On Saturday night we all went to a hockey game at the Wagon Wheel, then came back just to sit around and sing and share what the Lord had been doing in our lives. It was really great to open up like that with kids I'd never met before. I saw how Christ's love could be incorporated into my relationships with all people, even strangers.

Then, about the time I'd think I was really maturing, I'd do something stupid that would make my folks have to discipline me again. I went wheeling into Guilford in a hurry one morning and decided I could get away with parking in a no-parking zone. When I came back, sure enough, I had a ticket.

I drove to the drug store and showed it to my dad. He said, "Okay, you figure out when you can come in and work behind the counter. I'll pay you $1.25 an hour so you can pay the fine." I did it, too.

I started putting some of these conflicts and feelings down on paper around this time. I began writing prayers as a way to keep from falling asleep or letting my mind wander while I was praying. One night I wrote:

I'm very different-feeling tonight. I guess I'm tired, but also my relationship and sharing with my parents could be 100% better. I love them a whole bunch, and they have done for us kids (not selfishly) so much, and they have probably fulfilled Your plan. I pray that they will keep growing through You opening new doors for them, as You have for us through them. Help them to understand the freedom in a person that comes from knowing You are always guiding them. I agree, I haven't been as respectful as I should, but I guess maybe I'm trying (unconsciously) to show them this *real freedom*. Now that I'm thinking about it, maybe I (the human I, not the Christian I) was trying to illustrate this to them alone without Your help. Maybe this is just an excuse my brain made up for acting the way I have, but Lord, whatever it is, please just help

75

me, or someone else, to show them how I feel.

. . . Help mom and dad know how to approach us radical teen-agers so as not to turn us off. I pray that they get turned on to Your freedom and love down deep in the soul. I pray that our family will become more of a soul truth rather than fight it out to the end where nothing is accomplished.

A half-week later I wrote:

Be with mom and dad as they struggle to understand us. Help the good times of understanding to be so good that the bad ones don't even stand out (maybe that was dumb to ask for, but anyway).

11
asking for
the right ticket

Around the start of my senior year, it didn't look like I
was going to make it. Mr. Nielsen talked to my folks and
said, "Would you be very upset if Janet graduated in August
instead of June? I'm not sure we can get all the credits in."

We decided that would be all right if necessary, but it
sure would be nice to finish with all my friends.

Sometimes it didn't look like I was going to make it in
skating, either. By now the first stages of boredom had
set in. One night Miss Kohout took me to dinner at the
Wagon Wheel to say, "I want to know how you feel, so I'll
know how to go about teaching you. If you want to do well,
Janet, you have to put everything into it. If you really
want to keep going, if you're really interested, then I'm
still really interested in helping you. But if not, let's not
waste time."

She wasn't saying, "Do you want to win the Olympics

in '72?" She was saying, "Do you really want to skate?"
There's an important difference.

I knew what she meant. We were talking about
whether I wanted more years of six to eight hours a day
on ice. During full training when I wasn't in school, it
meant skating so hard that I'd fall into bed no later than
nine in the evening and sometimes as early as seven.

I said yes, I really did want to skate. I felt like the Lord
wanted me to continue, and down deep I still really loved
skating.

By Christmastime, I had myself together enough even to
write a poem. A friend named Diane Fons was at my house
one night, and I had walked her halfway home. It was
snowing, and the two of us stood like a couple of little
kids, staring up into a street light and watching the flakes
come plunging down into our open mouths. When I got
back to the house, I simply had to write:

Snow is so fantabulous!
Just think,
    God's love comes down with
        each snowflake to be with us
        for a while on earth.
    Snow eventually disappears
        but it will always come
        again with the right conditions.

Maybe that's why it's nice to have a white Christmas.
Just think,
    God's love came down with Jesus, too,
        to be with us for a while on earth.
    Jesus eventually disappeared
        but He is coming again
        with the right conditions as proclaimed by Him
        during His life on earth.

Only one difference that I can think of right now—
Just think,

Jesus brought God's perfect love into the world
   and it's *always* here somewhere
   and snow isn't always here somewhere,
   but then again,
   maybe it is in other parts of the world!
How real and beautiful!

Our family always worked together in the drug store on Christmas Eve so dad's employees wouldn't have to. It was always a riot, eating homemade Christmas cookies and breads and joking around until finally there were no more customers. Then we'd go home for a regular Christmas dinner, open our gifts, and then go to church at eleven o'clock for the candlelight service—and fall asleep! Everyone of us. Dad even snored one year.

On Christmas Day 1970 I wrote about something I'd mulled over all through high school:

It is funny how
   Realness and
   fakeness
can be felt between people.

I think, maybe,
   Realness is
everything done in love and
   fakeness is
everything else.

So . . .
Realness
   is felt with fullness and completeness,
     and
   fakeness is not really felt because it is
     emptiness and uncompleteness.

I had to put those nice words into practice about then with a girl at school named Wendy. We'd been friends as sophomores—until we started liking the same guy.

We hadn't spoken to each other in a year and a half. I went to her house one day and said, "Look, let's forget

79

all this. I want to be your friend, and I'd like you to forgive me for turning you off all this time."

Wendy was open, and we prayed together and got everything straightened out. After that, we didn't see each other very often, but it seemed like each would always pop in on the other at a strategic time, when one of us needed help and encouragement.

It was even harder to be real when I got to nationals in Buffalo at the end of January. Everyone expected me to win again, and reporters were trying to build the rivalry between me and Julie Holmes. I'd always done better than her at nationals while she'd always outplaced me at worlds, it seemed. I tried to explain that we were really close friends. By this time we had discovered that we both were Christians, along with Jo-Jo Starbuck, the pair-skating partner of Ken Shelley. We'd had some great times sharing and praying on tours.

After figures, it took the accountants two hours to figure out that Julie was slightly ahead. In my program that year, I had started to perfect a triple toe loop. The last thing Miss Kohout said as I went on the ice was, "If you miss the triple, don't worry about it."

Well, I missed the triple. I wasn't really in shape for a blazing four-minute program, but I still managed to pull it out. Everyone seemed to think I skated better after the fall, and I kept the championship.

That night—actually, early the next morning, I wrote a prayer:

Lord,
What didn't I do right?
  Where did I go wrong?
Can I do better?
  Please help me to have faith and not to doubt.
I know I can do it better next week
  with Your help
    whatever I need to do to do it better.

There are so many opportunities for me,
  but . . .
    where are they?

what are they?
please guide me to them.

I want to keep growing
    and growing
        and growing
and giving
    and giving
        and giving
and living
    and living
        and living
and forgiving
    and forgiving
        and forgiving
and loving
    and loving
        and loving.

The next evening the winners had to do an exhibition. Miss Kohout wouldn't let me do an easier program; she said, "Do the same one as last night, and do it right this time." I did.

Before we left Buffalo, there was a meeting of all of us on the team going to worlds, which were in Lyon, France, at the end of February. The officials explained that the 1971 North Americans to be held the very next week in Peterborough, Ontario, were optional. No one had to go, and if you thought you needed to rest and start getting ready for Lyon, do it.

Julie left on a trip to Japan. I felt like I should defend my North American title, though, and so we went.

I could tell the minute I walked into the arena that there was no way for me to win again. I could just sense it in the air—the whole place was buzzing with "Karen this—" and "Karen that—."

I had to skate each figure first, with Karen following me immediately. My first figures were really good; after three of them I was ahead by a slim 1.9 points. But then I began slipping. Karen told a Canadian reporter, "I knew I was coming on strong and got more confident with each

figure. I beat her in the worlds in Yugoslavia last year and I'm sure I can do it again this year." She did.

The next day I wrote:

Why,
why doesn't it bother me?
I guess because I'd rather live eternally
than win a stupid competition.

I'm so much happier when I'm in the trance of being myself and living from the inside out.
Force subdues; love wins!

I didn't think up that last line myself; it came from Miss Kohout, and it really helped me.

A week later, somewhere between Peterborough and Lyon, I copied down this "Twenty-third Psalm for Busy People" from a book:

The Lord is my pacesetter, I should not rush.
He makes me stop and rest for quiet intervals.
He provides me with images of stillness
   Which restore my serenity.
He leads me in ways of efficiency
   Through calmness of mind
   And His guidance is peace.
Even though I have a great many things
   To accomplish each day,
I will not fret, for His presence is here.
His timelessness, His all-importance
   Will keep me in balance.
He prepares refreshment and renewal
   In the midst of my activity.
By anointing my mind with His oils of tranquility
   My cup of joyous energy overflows.
Surely harmony and effectiveness
   Shall be the fruit of my hours,
For I shall walk in the pace of my Lord
   And dwell in His house forever!

Sometime during the competitions, Miss Kohout got a suggestion from one of the USFSA people that maybe I should have some additional help with figures. She accepted this with a very open mind, and one day she said, "Janet, you really do need someone else's help. I am not totally sure of myself on figures, and I'd like you to work a few days with Pierre Brunet in New York." I said, "Fine."

Pierre Brunet moved here from France a long time ago; he and his wife won the Olympic gold medal in pairs in both 1928 and 1932. He coached both Carol Heiss and Don Jackson, and he's about the nicest, most patient gentleman you could ever want to meet. He taught me some new things about figures that I'd never realized, some of the technical aspects.

When I got to Lyon, I got an encouraging letter from Glenn:

> Dear Janet,
> Hope this gets to you. Mom didn't give me much of an address. With all the help you got in New York you should do pretty good on figures. Are you going to put in your triple? I imagine it depends on the circumstances. Just remember, if you have to put it in to catch up, you have to have confidence that you can land it. If you mess it up, it's better just to drop it and put your other jump in. You still have another year to perfect it! If you do it, it's because *you're going to land it,* not try to land it, OKAY?

He went on with more paragraphs about pushing on in spite of how the judging goes. Then he closed with:

> Wrestling is going good. I've won the last five matches and I have the last dual meet tomorrow night. (I've pinned the guy once.) The Big Eight is next weekend . . . . *Just do your best and I'll do my best.* I will go to nationals this year, though. Maybe you can come to my nationals for once.

I was doing lots of thinking that practice week in Lyon. I got going one day on what it means to be "in love." I wrote:

> It makes me happiest when someone can see love in me and find out what makes it real and return the love, but go on living their life and me go on living mine. I guess I don't want this earthly love now because I'm only seventeen. I want to keep

moving on. Some girls say they want to find a guy, get married, and *settle down,* but somehow that's not my dream right now. Why settle down when there's so much life to be lived? I'm not happy stationary (at the same people's level all the time). I've got to look up to God and people He's spoken through on earth and to bigger goals. Like Bob Richards said, "A kid with a dream is a kid with a future."

My future I do not know, except that it will be hard, fun, rewarding, and God is taking care of all the different tickets to different tracks on the way to Eternal Life. He is standing at each gate with two tickets. One ticket is for the track leading nowhere and the other is the one for the track leading to Eternal Life. All one has to do is ask Him for the ticket to His Special Place.

It is impossible to understand God, though, and walk from gate to gate alone, so Christ walks with you and is your interpreter . . . . The Holy Spirit makes Christ come through the vault that holds love in each person. The Holy Spirit has an unknown formula for melting down the strongest vaults, so why try to do it ourselves? Imagine how rich we could all be if we could get to each other's vaults full of love!

The French press was doing all kinds of speculation that I'd win at worlds. But they were writing from their emotions, not the facts. At the end of the first day of figures I really messed up a paragraph double three.

That night I wrote:

I didn't have complete faith today
   especially on the last figure, Lord
      so there was no way—
I didn't even have complete faith in myself,
      let alone You—
   or
You—let alone myself.
Help me to have enthusiasm—and enthusiasm
   motivated by love—Your love.

On Saturday came the free skating. I was in fifth place after figures. Gabrielle Seyfert had retired by now, and Trixi Schuba had the lead. She was more controlled than ever. In

85

A.

Karen Magnussen (l.), *Trixi Schuba* (r.), *and I*
teasing a French gendarme *at the 1971 worlds in Lyon.*

figures, the circle will come out just right if you lean your
body at the right angle. When Trixi starts around that circle,
she's just like a ball on the end of a string. Her foot never
wobbles.

That Saturday, I skated really well. I didn't do the triple
toe loop, but put in a double lutz instead. I still felt good about
it. When the announcement came, it was Trixi Schuba in
first, Julie in second, Karen third, and me fourth. The ten
thousand Frenchmen started booing. While the medals were
being presented, they were chanting, "Lynn! Lynn! Lynn!"
It was really embarrassing. I finally had to go to the edge of the
ice and wave.

They were still booing Trixi the next afternoon at the
exhibition because of her rather ordinary free skating. That's
the trouble with the crowd not seeing the figures part of the
competition; they don't realize what happened before they got
there. The truth is that some very cruel things have been said
about Trixi. She's a very nice, quiet person, and all she's done
is play by the rules.

The 1971 tour of champions again went all over Europe: Grenoble, Moscow, Leningrad, Helsinki, East Berlin, Halle, Karl-Marx Stadt, Prague, Graz, Ljubljana, London, Geneva, Dortmund, and Cologne. I kept thinking the whole trip about Russia, because it related to my own struggle over a disciplined life. I wrote:

> Communism could be good in one way, in that it is a form of discipline for every person that lives by it—an organized discipline . . . that somehow we lack in the U.S. as a whole nation. We have more meaning to life because we find our own meaning, whereas I think communists are given their meaning to life . . . and have no way of experiencing things to find their own. They must live just to do their job for their country, and to exist. Without religion this is all they can do . . . .
>
> Many of us aren't *told* to do anything or suffer the consequences like the communists are. They just go through the motions through discipline outside of themselves. We must find an inner discipline to succeed which gives deeper meaning to life than an outer discipline. God helps us find this inner discipline which helps us be freer on the outside . . . . Therefore communists aren't as free as the ones who find this inner discipline which makes them *really* free.
>
> Thank you, thank you
>   Lord
> That I'm free
> and my parents have brought me up
>   from their outer discipline
> and shown me how to achieve
>   my own inner discipline
> so I'm *really free*, not just free!

12
on to sapporo

Somehow the rumor got started in the press that I couldn't graduate because I didn't have enough physical education credits. It made a nice story: Nasty old school officials won't let Janet Lynn, national skating champion, graduate because she hasn't been in gym enough.

The only trouble was, it wasn't true!

The school board, in fact, had waived all my P.E. requirements way back when I was a sophomore. They were really kind, in light of the fact that they'd never done that except for handicapped students.

When the rumor kept popping up in article after article, the board took a second step and *gave* me two P. E. credits. I didn't need them for P. E., so I just counted them as two more electives. And when my transcript was complete, it turned out I didn't need them at all; I graduated in June with two extra credits.

And high school ended kind of nice. I'm sure I could have

done better if I hadn't been skating, but as it was I ranked number 202 in a class of 614 and had a 2.7083 grade point average ("A" is 4.0). The night I was inducted into the National Honor Society Mr. Nielsen called me "Rockford's most traveled citizen." I even got some kind of "girl athlete of the year" award—which was really funny, considering how clumsy I am off the ice. I was always tripping down steps, dropping my books, falling in the hallway. Everyone always kidded me about it.

I'll never forget commencement—I was so relieved to be finally done. It was outdoors in the stadium, and the wind was blowing so hard we couldn't keep our hats on. But it was fun to be graduating with all my friends.

When it was over, I felt suddenly alone, like so many graduates do, I'm sure. I caught Mr. Nielsen at his car, grabbed his arm, and asked, "What am I going to do without school to go to?"

Some of the things I did without school that summer were:

—get fat (as always).

—skate exhibitions on the weekends (as always).

—counsel a cabin of seventh- and eighth-grade girls back up at Camp Augustana for a week. It was really a challenge not only to get them to stop thinking of me as Janet Lynn and get to know *me*, but also to identify in a normal way with kids so much younger than I. I led the nightly cabin devotions and also got to witness to some of them individually on the side.

My sister Carol was there that week, and it was the first time in a long time that the two of us got close. We both began admitting some of the hard feelings that had crept in, especially how hard it was for her to have to follow me. We both talked with Pastor about it before the week was out and learned how to express love to each other a little better. This didn't solve everything, but it was a start.

Pierre Brunet decided to bring all his students out from New York that summer to skate at the Wagon Wheel. So again we went to work on figures. He helped me understand more about what caused what—my figures really improved and I wasn't so nervous about them. I even began enjoying them at times!

Mr. Brunet also began teaching Gordie McKellen, which was the first time he'd agreed to teach a male skater since his own son, a very good skater, had been killed years ago in a car accident at the age of seventeen. By the end of the summer, Miss Kohout and all of us kids had talked Mr. Brunet into leaving the congestion of New York and staying a year in the rolling hills of northern Illinois. He's never gone back!

That fall, I left for Colorado College, promising Miss Kohout that I'd keep skating at the Broadmoor nearby. A lot of skaters —Peggy Fleming, Julie Holmes, and others—have taken advantage of the college's block calendar (one course at a time, six to eight weeks long) to keep skating.

I enrolled in a course in Christian ethics, which was way over my head. I also had a dance class on the side. At the end of the first block, I returned to Rockford to go into serious training for the Olympics. If any Olympiad were to be my peak, it had to be this one.

I can hardly remember the 1972 nationals in Long Beach, except that I won again, and that Margie came from Arizona to see me. She said the Lord had impressed her to skip lunch and spend the time in prayer for Gordie and for me. She'd been doing this for two weeks.

Back in Colorado Springs late that month, I worked so hard on the ice that I became exhausted. Suddenly I found myself in bed on doctor's orders for forty-eight hours. I bounced back pretty fast, though, and soon we were on our way to Japan.

I knew what Americans expected from me: the gold medal. I also knew how hard that would be to get. *Newsweek* pushed the dream along by putting me on the cover of their February 14 issue, but in the inside story they faced the facts:

In figure skating, American contenders are traditionally forced into the role of slow-starting race horses. After dropping far behind the early pace, they must rush into contention in the final strides—and do so with dazzling, twisting leaps. This often proves crowd-pleasing, but it is also nerve-wracking; the reason it happens is that this exquisitely esthetic, soaring sport is governed by a tiresomely bookish set of rules. Compulsory, or "school," figures count exactly as much as the daring, imaginative free skating; and in the compulsory figures, which are the first contested, the Americans are constantly outperformed by more disciplined rivals. Thus Harvard's John Misha Petkevich will probably perform his heart-grabbing free figures—the best in the world—in vain, because the school figures will have left him too far behind to have a chance.

Then there is Janet Lynn, a virtual cinch to enchant the Sapporo audiences with her dazzling free skating—and almost equally certain to fall short of the points accumulated by Austria's Beatrix Schuba in the dull compulsory competition . . . .

Sapporo, in the northernmost island of Japan called Hokkaido, was beautifully white with snow. I stayed with Jo-Jo and Barbara Brown in a room in the Olympic Village. Again there were the thrilling opening ceremonies, even better than at Grenoble because this time I was well and could enjoy them to the fullest.

Ladies' skating came fairly early in the schedule; the first day of figures was Friday, February 4. I felt really good. I said, "Well, Lord, I just want to do my best. Please help me." And I went out and did three really good figures—the counter, the paragraph three, and the rocker. One judge, Mr. Obitani of Japan, even had me first on the counter instead of Trixi, which was a shock. When the points were totaled, I was third.

I went back to the room that night and began praying. My prayer was, "Okay, Lord, if I can do that good tomorrow—even a little better—maybe I can win this thing . . . for You." I sort of tacked that "for You" on the end because I knew I should.

But the Lord knew what I really meant!

I was slipping into the "I want to beat" attitude.

The next day's figures were the paragraph double three,

the change loop, and the paragraph bracket. The first one went pretty good.

But the change loop simply fell apart. It was terrible. My marks were from 3.9 all the way down to 3.4. Trixi, by contrast, scored from 4.4 up to 4.8, and by the end of the day had an overwhelming lead. I was fourth.

I dodged the reporters and went back to my room shattered. Through my tears I said, "Lord, *why*? I wanted to do this for You, and I thought You wanted me to win . . . ." Both mom and Miss Kohout tried to calm me down.

The Lord let me cry for a while, and when I was finally ready to listen He seemed to say, "I still love you. I love you regardless of how you skate. Don't worry about the medal; you're not skating for the medal, you're skating for Me."

My mind went back to what my counselor had said at confirmation camp 4½ years before: "Jesus is living inside you all the time now. Whenever you fail or feel inferior, just give those feelings to Him."

I began to relax. I started letting my negative feelings sort of float away from me toward the ceiling. It was like being loosened from a vise. I lay there praying for a long time, getting my attitudes back where they belonged, listening to what Christ was telling me through my thoughts.

After practicing Monday morning, I had the whole day in front of me before the competition that night. I said, "Okay, Lord, I'm going to forget about everything, and I just ask you to give me the right feelings at the right time."

Did He ever! When I stepped on the ice that night in front of eight thousand people, the most unusual thing happened. I was skating around in a little circle waiting for the announcement of the previous girl's marks . . . when it seemed like God's love just came down all over me like a blanket. I've never in my life felt anything so wonderful. It was as if He was saying, "I love you, and just be filled with My love and go out there and skate because you love it."

It was such an experience—I'll never forget it. I think I could have fallen twenty times after that, and it wouldn't have bothered me!

I went whirling into my program, enjoying every step of

it, pouring out this love I had received to the crowd. I felt God's power in the reaction I was getting—I knew that in myself I simply couldn't do that to an audience. Christopher Brasher, a writer for the *London Observer,* sensed it too, I think; he later wrote:

> Her performance here on Monday night when she won the free skating was one of those rare occasions when sport is lifted into the realms of art. She did not win a gold medal but that is only because the world is an unjust place.
>
> . . . There is a movement in her program . . . when she suddenly moves backwards so that her blonde hair flies forward and her arms are outstretched and she is indeed a young girl in love with the world. She would say she is thanking God for so much happiness. Those who watch her can make of it what they will, knowing only that it is supremely beautiful.

Then, all at once, it happened. I went into a flying sit-spin— which is pretty easy; I'd done them in competitions for years, and never messed one up. And suddenly I wasn't spinning.

I was sitting on the ice!

A reporter asked me later, "What did you *really* think about at that moment?"

And I had to tell him: "I just thought about getting up!"

I guess the whole world groaned when I fell. People all over the world were watching on television, of course, and they couldn't believe that Janet Lynn had fallen in free skating. People who assumed I still had a chance for the gold medal were doubly shocked.

I didn't have time to be shocked. All I knew was that the double axel was next, and I hopped up and did it. Then came a slow part, and that's when it dawned on me what I'd just done.

God's presence was not about to be dispelled by a little fall, however. I skated the rest of my program with the same smile on my face, enjoying it as much as I had the first part.

Free skating is judged in two parts: technical merit and artistic impression. For technical merit I got seven 5.9s and two 5.8s. For artistic impression I got six 5.9s, two 5.8s and a perfect 6.0 from Mr. Lago, a Swedish judge who had been one of the toughest on me during figures. I couldn't believe it—a 6.0 for artistic impression, in spite of a fall!

Miss Kohout and I studied the videotape later and figured out what happened. I had taken a jump combination at the wrong angle, which sent me into an axel at the wrong angle. So in order to get to the right position for the sit-spin, I had to sort of turn a corner. I curved into the spin instead of taking it straight, and lost my footing.

When all the points were totaled, Trixi had 2,751.5, Karen had 2,673.2, and I had 2,663.1. Julie was really nervous for her free skating and came in fourth with 2,627.0.

I stood there on the awards stand and was nothing but happy as I accepted my huge, two-inch-wide bronze medal. I knew I had done what the Lord wanted me to do that night.

Of course we had to skate an exhibition the next night, which was even more fun. I was beseiged by sportswriters for the rest of the Olympics, and the question was always the same, "How could you get up and smile after you fell?" Talk about the perfect opportunity to tell about Christ in my life!

Sometimes they even asked about the way I was signing autographs: "Peace † Love, Janet Lynn." I told how at first I'd signed "Best Wishes" like everybody else, but it seemed shallow to me. I tried some others. "Happiness Always" took too long to write. I couldn't find what I wanted.

So one day I took time to think: What do I really wish for people? Well, peace . . . and love. It was short and very meaningful to me. That became my autograph. I turned the *and* into the form of the Cross, although I don't think that dawns on most people.

And when I'm not mobbed, I take time to say a silent prayer for each person as I sign it.

The hallway of our Olympic Village room started filling up with mail each day, which brought on a lot of kidding from Jo-Jo and Barbara. When the day came to leave, they said, "Why don't you sign your name on the wall and give somebody a big thrill? They'll repaint it anyway."

Kishimoto

Above: *Marching to the final ceremonies of the '72 Olympics in Sapporo.* Below: *Rockford's proud welcome.*

So I found a felt-tip marker and scrawled big letters over the door, "Peace † Love! Janet Lynn USA 1972 Ladies 3rd place (figure skating)."

Later, when the Japanese turned the Olympic Village into permanent apartments, I guess they had a big discussion about whether to repaint that wall. The family moving in all wanted it left alone except the mother, who finally gave in!

13
coming off
the mountain

Rockford, as you might expect, threw the biggest celebration yet when I got home. They sent a special bus to O'Hare to pick me up. There were twelve hundred people packed into the Rock Valley College fieldhouse waiting for me on a Tuesday afternoon. Even Guilford's stage band was there to play the national anthem.

Welcomes have always been hard times for me to be honest. One time flying home from Europe I started rambling on a piece of hotel stationery:

> How can I be real to all the people at home if they meet us at the airport if I don't *really* want to play up to them? I want to see all my friends that know me but not all the people who have visions of me skating. If I cry, it's because I miss all the kids—not because I'm glad to be brought back home by a bunch of people. But why do I feel this way . . .
>
> Why do I only like being appreciated *away* from home?

I want to be myself when I get home (Chicago or wherever) but how, Lord, how? . . . I need to be guided on the right road to peace between people. Help the tension to leave me and to be myself no matter what, to think what I *truly* feel before I act or speak.

I have never been scared to go home before—why am I now? I don't know what home is expecting me to be and I am afraid that I have changed a *lot* from what I used to be—will they like it? . . . I'm a sinner—help them to know it!

I was probably too tired to do that much thinking about this homecoming. Everyone knew I'd just flown across the Pacific, and the program was kept to a half-hour. Pastor Peterson was the emcee. I did a lot of crying, but I also managed to be fairly open about the Lord this time, even though it was a mixed group of people. I said, "The glory has to go to God, because He's the one who made all this possible."

I was in bed by five P.M.!

As soon as I got rested, though, I was back in training for the worlds coming up in March in Calgary. It took a while to recuperate from the time change, and I don't think many of the Olympic skaters were really "up" for the worlds. The results came out exactly the same: Schuba, Magnussen, Lynn, in that order.

The four-week tour ran from one side of the continent to the other: Edmonton, Winnipeg, Detroit, Toronto, Montreal, Ottawa, Philadelphia, New York, Halifax, Quebec, Saint Paul, Vancouver, Seattle, Oakland, and Los Angeles. In New York we got to meet Kurt Waldheim, secretary general of the United Nations, and we also heard Norman Vincent Peale preach at Marble Collegiate Church; I'd read some of his books.

The best memories, though, are of the kids themselves. My copy of the official tour program is filled with their signatures and notes wishing me good luck and friendship—some in English, some in German, some in Russian. On the page listing all the past world champions, somebody even scribbled in "1973—Bratislava—Janet Lynn." Jo-Jo's words take up the whole back cover.

At the end of tour, my mom and I were in the Los Angeles airport waiting to catch a plane for Phoenix so we could see Margie and rest a few days. A lady walked up with two little girls, about eight and five, and asked, "Are you Janet Lynn?"

I said yes.

"Oh, my daughters just love you so much." Here we go again, I thought. "They watch you every time you're on TV, and they recognized you right away. They just think you're so wonderful—could you possibly give them your autograph? Oh, that would just be the grandest thing!"

So I signed an autograph for them. She kept right on talking, "Oh, thank you, thank you—they'll treasure this all of their lives!"

As they walked away, we were snickering—but we really cracked up when one of the little girls looked up and said, "Who was that, mommy?"

Margie was having a good year at Arizona State, and it was refreshing to relax with her. I was feeling kind of down, and we spent a lot of time reading the Scripture and praying together. One night it was really gorgeous, and so we went outdoors to pray.

She had told me about this church she'd been attending which taught a lot about the work of the Holy Spirit. I'd heard about the Holy Spirit all my life, studied Him in confirmation class right alongside Margie, and all that. But these people believed that the New Testament description of the "the baptism with the Holy Spirit," where He came and seemed to fill Christians with His love and power and even caused them to speak in unknown languages, wasn't just a fluke. They had Margie convinced that this was a genuine spiritual experience that made you more useful to Christ.

So this night, while we were praying, Margie did something very normal for her: she began to pray in "tongues"—this language that the Holy Spirit had given her.

It really scared me. I moved about twenty feet away from

her. I had no idea what she was saying, and something about it just unnerved me.

Then I thought, "Well, she says it's from God, and if it is, I shouldn't be afraid of it." I prayed, "Lord, I need You to help me now. If this is from You, help me to accept it and get rid of this fear."

Naturally, I told Margie my impressions while we walked back to her room, and she tried to tell me that there was nothing to fear, that it was all explained there in the Bible. She said she had wanted to pray for me, but didn't really know how, so she'd let the Holy Spirit do it through her.

Back in Rockford, the whirlwind of congratulations and compliments continued. One of the few places I could be an ordinary person was at the rink. The kids there have always accepted me as just another skater, probably because Miss Kohout never made a big fuss over me. She never put my picture up after a competition or in any way made me a celebrity. She wanted to keep the rink as my second home so I would always feel comfortable coming there. I can't thank her enough for that.

One day that summer, the ice was melted, and so we had all the kids from the skaters' dorm down to our house to swim. On the way back to Rockton, we were all jammed into Mike's van and Rick's Volkswagen bug—probably nineteen of us in all.

We were in a really goofy mood. At the stoplight beside Northtown Shopping Center, we decided to have a Chinese fire drill and exchange cars at the same time. The kids from the bug made it fine into the van, but the dozen kids from the van all tried to fit into the bug and it was really wild—arms and legs hanging out all over!

All of this was in a sense a cover-up for the tension that was building inside me. The kids knew, though, what was going on; there was no way I could hide my feelings once I got on the ice. In spite of the smiles in public, the old eagerness was gone. Then came the August morning when I drove back home and made my announcement that skating was all over.

14

a little help
from a friend

Mom just stared at me. I was nineteen years old; she couldn't force me to go on, and she wouldn't have if she could have. She asked what had happened.

We began to talk about it. I poured out a lot of my frustration. Her only advice was, "Well, this is the wrong time of year to quit. You're already halfway to another competition season—why not stick it out?"

The rest of the day I spent talking to people: mom and dad, Glenn, Pastor Peterson—and Miss Kohout for three hours. We decided I was spending too much time on the ice and that I should just forget the regimen for a while. She said, "Until two months before competition, why don't you just skate when you feel like it? If you're bored, get off the ice and go home. Do something else. See if that doesn't help your attitude toward the whole thing."

I said okay—I'd keep skating on that basis. I slacked off quite a bit. I spent only about two or three hours a day on figures and an hour on free skating. One weekend I just took off and went to see some friends; I didn't tell Miss Kohout or anyone at the rink I was going, which was a real switch. I also got more involved in answering my mail.

Late in August my mom, Carol, and I were driving to Colorado Springs for the Broadmoor Ice Show, leaving early on a Sunday morning. Nancy Oldenburg called Saturday all excited; she *had* to see me about something. But she had to go to dinner with her parents that evening. I said, "Well, I'm leaving for Colorado in the morning."

"Then can I come over after I'm back from dinner?"

So at sometime after eleven o'clock I found myself listening to Nancy spill out her story.

"You remember one Sunday after church when you told me about Margie's thing with tongues, and how you were afraid she was going off the deep end?"

I said yes. We had both been rather critical, saying things like, "Does she think she's better than us now? We don't need anything that's going to make us proud spiritually."

Nancy went on. "Well, this friend of mine called the other night really turned on because she'd just had the same experience. I listened to all her excitement and asked a bunch of questions. And then I really couldn't get to sleep that night thinking about it.

"The more I thought about it, the more afraid I became."

I told Nancy that's how I'd felt listening to Margie.

She said, "It felt like Satan was actually there in my bedroom—and I knew I had to do something. I had to either ask for this infilling of the Holy Spirit or else give in to fear."

So she asked for the Holy Spirit to come and take over completely. Her fear left. "It seemed like a soft wind just sort of filled the room and surrounded my body on all sides," she said. She could tell that God was in the room now, not Satan. And then she began to speak in tongues.

"And Janet, it was so great, because I knew I was praising God and thanking Him for all He's done for me—only much more effectively, because the Holy Spirit was giving the words."

I was stunned. Two of my best friends.

For the next hour and a half Nancy and I talked. She showed me in *Acts* in the New Testament the experiences of Christians in the first century. She said it wasn't anything spooky; it was just a greater measure of control by the Holy Spirit, which meant greater power in sharing Christ with people and in living like we should. She said she loved everyone so much more now—even people she hadn't liked before!—because God's love had filled her.

Finally, at about one o'clock, I said, "Nancy—would you pray for me?"

She blurted out, "Why do you think I came over here?!"

She prayed. She prayed for me to be open to whatever the Holy Spirit wanted to do in my spiritual life.

Then I prayed. I said, "Lord, I don't know what this is all about, but I really do want the power of the Holy Spirit in my life. Take me and use me."

I began making sounds—syllables. It was obviously me doing the speaking, only it wasn't English. And it wasn't Spanish, which I'd studied for three years in high school and almost forgotten already. It was a language given by the Holy Spirit.

I had never felt such joy overwhelming me. Before long, I was laughing while Nancy was crying. It was so neat to be giving God the praise that He really deserved in a way unlimited by my little vocabulary.

I couldn't wait to share all of this with a couple of girls I had gotten to know in Colorado Springs, Susan and Linda Lichty. They were both students at Oral Roberts University in Tulsa and had received this baptism, too.

I wanted to share it with my family as well, but the truth is that I didn't go about it in the right way. It was obvious that I still had problems, especially my struggle with skating. The Holy Spirit didn't suddenly straighten everything out for me.

I began spending more and more time at church. Some of the people there had received this experience back in the spring and had begun a Thursday night Bible study. Some of them were meeting afterwards for prayer in the sanctuary, and the gifts of the Spirit (as described in *I Corinthians*) were being permitted. Pastor Peterson had been Spirit-filled even earlier, I found out, but he insisted that laymen should lead the Thursday meetings so long as they stayed true to the Scriptures.

I began learning a lot on Thursday nights, especially the biblical foundation for what had happened to me. I found out that this was simply a greater measure of what I already had as a result of salvation. I also learned that there was a lot of controversy about this "charismatic renewal" of the churches, as it was called. But they said, "You don't have to speak in another language—you *get to!* It releases something inside you, and you know that God is doing it, since you can't do it by yourself."

I probably talked too much about all this at home without showing my family the love that should go along with it. At one point I think my folks were concerned about me just like I had been about Margie. They even asked Pastor if he didn't think I was getting a little too wrapped up in church, prayer meetings, and Bible study, and wasn't as well-rounded as I should be. He, having been to the Lutheran International Conference on the Holy Spirit in Minneapolis that summer, assured them that this renewal was a good thing and that I'd mature a little more before long.

Everything would have been a lot better if I would have let the Holy Spirit help me with my chronic rebellion against my parents' authority. I was spending a lot of time alone in my room, reading my Bible or just sleeping, because I didn't know what to do with all my time. My mom got really upset because I wasn't doing anything constructive, she thought. She wanted me to give more attention to growing mentally and physically, and she was right.

That fall, I enrolled in two courses at Rockford College: English composition and world religions. I really enjoyed the English course, but I missed so much of the other one because of weekend exhibitions that I finally had to drop it.

The courses were a good diversion from skating, and so was my volunteer service at Rockford's juvenile home. I really enjoyed talking with girls who had hard lives without the opportunities I'd had, just getting to know them and love them and be their friend.

One night I got permission to take a girl who was about fifteen with me to a ladies' prayer circle where I was to speak. Wendy went with us, too. Everything went fine until the girl asked to use the phone. I didn't even think; I just said, "Sure—it's in the other room." She disappeared into the bedroom, and when Wendy went in there a little later, she was long gone out the window.

Panic! We all prayed for her, and soon I left to go tell the people at the juvenile home what had happened. They were much nicer about it than I had expected; they said, "Don't worry about it—it happens all the time."

By the time I had driven home, there was a message waiting to call the house where we'd been. The dear girl had begun to feel guilty and had come back!

Meanwhile, the Lord was helping me a little with my skating, but it was still drudgery. I kept telling the kids at the rink, "If I make it through this year, it'll be a *miracle*." I wasn't exaggerating. I felt like just *surviving*—getting through the competitions without coming unglued—would be a miracle of God.

And He knew how much I was struggling. Around November He sent Linda Lichty and a bunch of kids from ORU up to see me just to encourage me. Susan called me out of the blue one Friday and said, "Is it okay if we come up tomorrow? We just thought maybe you needed us."

I said, "Wow, do I ever! The only trouble is, I have to skate tomorrow night, but we can be together after that."

By the time they arrived, I had bad news: Miss Kohout had said we would listen to music over at her house after workout. (Choosing music for a free-skating program always took hundreds of hours.)

"Can't you get out of that?" Susan asked.

I said, "No—you don't cancel on Miss Kohout."

Susan said, "Well, we'll come watch you skate, and we're going to pray that you'll get out of the late part so we can spend some time together!"

At the end of workout, I went to Miss Kohout and said,

"Shall I come on over to your house now to listen to music?"

She said, "No, you don't have to come tonight—I've gotten behind on lessons and I have to teach now."

Well, that launched us into quite a time of sharing, singing, and praying back at my house! It was just what I needed. Sometime around midnight, my sister Carol and two friends—they'd all been drinking—came in. Carol was a sophomore now and was being influenced heavily by some school friends.

They hardly understood what we were doing. Naturally, I was embarrassed. They finally went on into her room and we continued worshiping the Lord informally.

Over Thanksgiving vacation, two ORU students came back. One of them, Alan, went to the skaters' dorm at the Wagon Wheel one evening and began sharing about Christ with a large group of kids. He reinforced what I'd been trying to share with two girls there. They had listened to me explain the Four Spiritual Laws and had said, "We buy everything but that last one. Personally inviting Christ into your life—that doesn't make sense. We don't have to pray to Christ to get to God."

Whenever I had said, "I just can't skate without the Lord—He really helps me," the one girl would go, "You're nuts. I don't see Him out there skating—I see you!"

The morning after the dorm gathering, she was on the ice and felt really rotten. Her jumps were terrible. And then, she told me later, "All of a sudden I was doing the most beautiful jumps like I hadn't done for a long time. I don't know what happened, but it was all at once, and I knew it was the Lord—I just knew it." She remembered what Alan had said the night before and became a Christian that day.

The other girl came to the Lord a few weeks later, at 11:53 on New Year's Eve! I wasn't there, but when I saw her the next morning at the rink, I said, "Happy New Year!" She got this funny grin and said, "Happier than you think!"

While she had been finding Christ, I had been writing a letter:

Dear Lord,

It's been a long time since I've written to You. I really don't know what to say. Lord, it's the last day of 1972—almost the last hour—praise You! It's been a good year in that I have learned more about You, but it's been a year of real trial for me, Lord. I know that I've done a lot of things wrong this year—so many things every day. I ask You to forgive me, Lord.

I really don't feel like I'm writing from deep down in my heart and soul. I guess I haven't examined my heart and soul. Well, last year is almost over and I thank You for my many blessings and I ask You to be with me more than ever as the year 1973 comes in. Lord Jesus, I love You as much as I ever have and I truly want to live my life the way You want me to. I truly don't want to be partial to anyone. I ask for the understanding of other people so that I can love them more and show them that I do. I ask that You teach me to love. I want to learn to love the way You love. I know I will never become as loving as You, but I know You can help me to learn to love.

Also, one big thing is that I really want to be able to control my temper. No matter what, I just ask You'll *never* let me get so mad that I lose my temper. I have faith that You will help me with that. Thank You, Lord! Please forgive me for my temper. I ask You to subdue it and teach me patience so that people will be able to see that I am a Christian by my actions. I don't want to turn anyone off to You. I don't want to be a show-off of my life, either. I don't want to make people think that I'm using Your forgiveness and my evil nature (imperfection) as an excuse for anything I do.

Lord, I want to serve You—no matter what I have to do. No matter what I do I want my motives to be right—my attitude to be a Christian one, by Scripture implanted in my being by the Holy Spirit.

Lord, I don't know what You have planned for my family, but I ask in a loving spirit that You will open my eyes to whatever my family tells me and I ask that You will open their eyes to Your great joy. Please forgive me for turning them off to You. Lord, You know I want to be an example, but I only can be by listening to You and Your Holy Spirit and *letting You* change me and mold me from the inside so I won't have to act superficial or so I won't have to have so much pressure on me. If I want to live a Christian life and only try by myself and I don't ask You to change me from the inside, I will get sick of it and tired and I won't be able to live that way. So, Lord, mold me the way You want me. My spirit is in Your almighty and loving hands. I thank You, Lord!

About skating this year and my future—it's all in Your

hands. I ask You right now to be able to "fight to win" *(I Corinthians 9:26)* and I ask that You will give me the strength to land my jumps *and* skate with Your love glowing through. "I can do all things through Christ who strengtheneth me" *(Philippians 4:13)*. I claim that, Lord, right now. You wanted me to compete again this year and I thank You for all Your mighty promises that we can claim as ours.

Lord, You also know that I have asked for all Your gifts of the Spirit—whatever ones You want me to have and when. Teach me how to obey Your Spirit. I don't want to miss out on anything You have planned for me. I want to be able to spread Your word, but please don't let me get so excited spreading the Good News that I forget to love. I love You, Lord, more than anything, and yet I hurt You. I can imagine how I hurt people on earth—especially my family. Jesus, You are the Great Healer; I ask You to send Your Spirit to heal all the hurts in our family. I ask You to make us all bow down to You in repentance all the time, and I ask that You will place faith in our hearts instead of doubt, and love instead of hate or envy or jealousy. I ask that we will all bow down in repentance and reverence to You, Lord—all of us together in Your great name, which has victory over death and our many trials. Thank you, Lord, for helping me to keep my head. I also ask You in the name of Jesus that Satan will be bound from our family and from any of our relationships with each other or other people. And then, Lord, help us to keep our eyes on You—the Giver—and not the gifts or trials or sorrows. Thank you, Jesus.

I want to pray for these people tonight, Lord. You know their needs, and please minister to those needs:

I then filled a sheet of notebook paper with two columns of names—everyone from grandpa to kids at the rink to Julie Holmes to Pastor to Miss Kohout to mom and dad to all kinds of other people. I finished off with:

Lord, thanks—good night, and thanks for the new year— be with all of us, please. Amen, in Christ's name!

108

Margaret S. Williamson

15
disaster

It was the middle of January before my 1973 free-skating program finally came together. I had quite a battle with resentment toward Miss Kohout for not working on it, until I succeeded in turning the whole thing over to the Lord.

I was fighting an even bigger battle with my weight. I was too heavy to compete and I knew it. My mother hadn't had her glasses changed for a while, and for a long time she thought I was slimmer than I really was (honest!). Then she got a new pair of glasses and realized how fat I was. So she helped me lose a little.

But people could tell that I wasn't skating my best. At nationals they'd come up to me and say things like, "Gee, I like your *dress!*"

And everyone expected me to do all the better this year because of the scoring change. The International Skating Union wasn't quite ready to go to a sixty-forty ratio in favor of free skating, but they did make it a little better. They set up three competition parts: (1) three school figures instead of six, which counted forty percent; (2) a compulsory short program (skating with music for two minutes or less and including certain required jumps)—twenty percent; (3) the regular four-minute free-skating program—forty percent.

Despite all of Mr. Brunet's work, I finished second in figures at Minneapolis.

My compulsory short program wasn't in much better shape than my regular one. I finished second again—but to a different girl.

That night, I really felt discouraged. It was another Sapporo experience—crying for three hours, telling the Lord, "I don't want to skate tomorrow night!" He really used my mom this time to talk me out of my negative feelings. She said, "If you have faith, all you have to do is ask God to help you when you skate—you should *know* He'll be there." The Lord reminded me that I was skating for Him and He gave me *His* peace.

The next night, while waiting to skate, I again felt that blanket of God's love come over me like I'd felt in Sapporo. I went out and skated a perfect program. It was my fifth year as women's national champion—and I finally got the Owens Memorial Trophy this time. It had been lost in the mail when Peggy Fleming sent it back or something, and so I hadn't received anything the first four times.

The 1973 North Americans were scheduled for Rochester, New York. Right at the last minute the Canadians asked that they be canceled. They said that the series didn't really serve a purpose anymore since most American and Canadian skaters were now getting lots of international experience in Europe other than at worlds.

It was fine with me. I needed all the time I could to get in better shape for Bratislava. The new rules were in my favor, Trixi Schuba had retired to skate with an ice show, and everyone thought the door was wide open for me to win the world championship. *Sports Illustrated* ran a feature story on me entitled, "This Is It, for Heaven's Sake," which you could take two different ways.

Gordie McKellen, who had become a Christian by this time,

had won the men's national championship. He and his mother, Miss Kohout, Mr. Brunet, mom, and I left two weeks early to train in Innsbruck, Austria. Miss Kohout wasn't pushing me nearly as hard this year (for obvious reasons); she knew I wasn't a little kid she could chase around the rink anymore. I skated from seven to noon each morning, working mainly on figures, and that was it.

I had brought along some tapes of teaching sessions by several different ministers—Bob Mumford, Don Basham, and Derek Prince. I spent a lot of time listening to these, and for the first time mom and I got into some really deep sharing on spiritual things.

I was trying to keep steady, trusting the Lord for whatever He wanted, as we arrived in Bratislava. I was especially praying for help to be a more joyful Christian. Meanwhile, the pressure began to build. A charter flight arrived from Rockford; it included my dad (who had a great time trying out his Polish on the Czechs!) and even Nancy (someone paid her way at the last minute).

The morning the school figure competition began, the rink was terribly cold. I was nervous and shivering, but that was nothing new for the start of figures. The first one, a counter, wasn't too bad.

The second one was a backward paragraph loop, which everybody hates. It has a quick little circle to be done inside the bigger circle. But I had been doing it really well in practice, sometimes within an inch all the way.

The last thing before I stepped on the ice, Miss Kohout said, "Janet, there are so many people praying for you today—I bet the lines are so jammed the Lord can't even get to them all!" It was so funny just at that moment, and so beautiful.

The ice was hilly, and dirty as well from the judges' shoes. I kept wandering around looking for a clean spot. Finally I started the figure. I was shaking from the very start, and it didn't turn out very good.

The final figure was a forward paragraph bracket, which I'd sometimes done well in practice—and sometimes not.

The first two times around, it was fantastic! The circles were perfectly round and the tracings were right on top of each

112

Miss Kohout and I at the difficult 1973 nationals.   Tom Peterson

other. As I pushed off for the third tracing, I thought, "Hey, this is really a good figure—" and that's what Mr. Brunet means by "letting go," easing up on your concentration for just a second. I looked down—and was horrified to find myself suddenly about fifteen inches off!

I immediately prayed, "Lord, help me relax—You take over." By the time I finished the six tracings, they looked pretty good except for the one bulge. In fact, it was still the best paragraph bracket I'd done in a competition.

When the points were announced, I was only slightly behind Karen in second place. I was pretty happy.

The next day when it was time to skate the compulsory short program, it seemed like the rink was even colder. My legs were freezing and I was really tense. Something about *having* to do certain jumps instead of doing what I felt just turned me off. I really had a mental block against it, I think.

I had to do a combination of two jumps somewhere in the program, and I'd planned a double axel/double toe loop. I had done it fine in Innsbruck, but during the daytime practice this day I couldn't do it at all. I must have tried it fifteen times. I was tempted to change it to a double toe loop/double toe loop, but then I said, "No. There's no reason why I can't do what I planned. I'm going ahead with it."

When my turn came that evening, I started the program and was very shaky on the first spin. I came to the combination and fell on the double axel. The longer I skated, the worse it got. By the time I got to the last double axel, I wasn't even thinking. I just threw myself into it—and fell for the second time in less than two minutes.

I'd never failed so completely in my life. Janet Lynn, world's greatest free skater—sprawled all over the ice. I kept trying to smile, but I was choking back the tears. I passed Dick Button on the way out, and he tried to make a joke by saying, "Well, I always told you that if you're going to do it good, do it really good!"

Both Miss Kohout and I burst into tears the minute we got inside the dressing room. I just fell into her arms and sobbed for a long time. Karen was there, and she was stunned. She kept repeating, "I can't believe it . . . I can't believe it. . . . Janet, I never wanted you to skate like that."

Jean Scott, a British skater, was there too, and began crying as she tried to comfort me. She said, "Janet, I'm really sorry . . . it's hard to take, isn't it?"

The compulsory short program totals were announced a little later. I was *twelfth*.

So this was what the hardest year of my life had come to.

16
decision time

Over the next twenty-four hours, the Lord did a lot of teaching. It was a new experience for me to be so humiliated, and only in this way could I learn how to get back up again. The next night while warming up, I felt exhausted, not only physically but emotionally. I knew I had to trust God more than ever to make it through my program.

I took it easy that night because I was tired. I just kept thinking, "I love this, I love this, I love this, and I want to show it," as I went through every move.

When it was over, I glided to the side, relieved. Jim McKay of ABC was standing there, and he put his arm around me as he said, "That was the hardest competition ever, wasn't it, Janet?"

I answered, "You better believe it!" It was neat to have him understand what I'd been going through.

In spite of my cautiousness, I got two 6.0s and was again first in free skating, which offset my other scores enough to give me the silver medal. Karen won the gold.

And I think that's the way the Lord wanted it. In fact, I know He didn't want me to win at Bratislava. Not because He's mean or anything, but because it would have ended my career too perfectly. People would have put me up on even a higher pedestal than they do now. But since I "failed," it's really interesting how much more I have been able to communicate with people who haven't done anything particularly outstanding in life.

People immediately began saying, "Janet, you've got to give it one more year. You just had a bad break; you'll win next year for sure." But I knew that if I skated another year, I'd be skating strictly for the medal. I'd never done that up to this point, and I wasn't going to start.

On Monday night I wrote:

> Some people would say that I'm using my faith as a cover-up for not winning this year and not going on. If I didn't really believe that this past year was the Lord's will and not competing anymore was the Lord's will, I could go on competing to win the gold medal in '74—because I *could* do it if that was my will or God's will. But a medal or world title is not what the Lord judges us by.
>
> Lord, I ask for Your guidance on tour to have fun, learn a lot, and skate with love radiating to the people. . . . Thank You for providing Nancy at worlds, and my dad and brother and aunt and uncle. I believe You had a purpose for every one of them. I thank You for the way I skated figures, short program, and four-minute. I thank You for getting me through the difficult times I had. I thank You for the offers I've had. I thank You that Miss Kohout loves me and is understanding and cares. I thank You that Mr. Brunet is so wonderful.
>
> Please help me to go home thinner than I've ever been, or as thin as I've ever been. Lord, that is a must, and I want to do it by being happy—not by punishing myself. Let me

make life a challenge instead of a pressure. Thank You, Lord! I love You! Use me to Your glory in love! In Jesus' name, Amen.

The professional offers were starting to come again, and one day while still in Bratislava, mom, Miss Kohout, and I went out to lunch with Dick Button and his associate to talk about it. Dick said, "Janet, do you want to skate professionally? If you do, I would be glad to represent you in negotiations with the ice shows."

The restaurant was busy, which made it kind of hard to talk, and I didn't feel like nailing anything down anyway. I said, "I think I want to, but I'm not sure. I talked it over with my family at Christmas, and they all said it was okay with them. But I've been trying to keep it out of my mind until after this competition."

We left it up in the air. I went on tour vacillating back and forth—yes one day, no the next. The rest of the kids knew what I was going through without my saying much. Some offered advice; I just listened.

Rick Talley summed up my dilemma about that time in a newspaper column (he'd moved now from Rockford to work for *Chicago Today*). He entitled it, "Now Is the Time for Janet to Quit," and part of it said:

> It's time for the young woman, Janet Lynn Nowicki, to make a decision. Perhaps she already has made it. Perhaps she has had her private conversation with God.
>
> Janet always has made her decisions with His help. She skates with the Lord and she counsels with Him.
>
> She has given her life to Him and to her quest for skating brilliance. . . .
>
> Janet, the girl, skated for the love of skating. Janet, the young woman, has learned there is more to life than an ice rink and runny nose. . . .
>
> Now, weary in mind and body, Janet must realize that she will be 22 in 1976 and she must realize a blade could slip then, too.
>
> Will she be able to quit without quite reaching the world pinnacle in world figure skating? As a friend and observer, do I really want to see her quit?
>
> I think so. I think it's time for Janet Lynn Nowicki to

move on to bigger things, on and off the ice. Her future, I think, lies in television.

Perhaps her decision already has been made. Whatever it may be, I'm confident she will be able to handle it.

With His help, of course. That's the way it is with Janet. What do you think they'll decide?

I had gone on tour with the condition that I could drop out at any point. If I got too tired, I wasn't going to push myself anymore. The tour officials understood that.

I almost quit after East Germany. The next stop was Russia, and I was really tempted to skip the rest and go home. Mom and I had a good talk that night, and I decided to stay on.

About a week later, we finished in Leningrad and took a night train to Helsinki, Finland. The next day when I went out to practice—all of a sudden, it happened.

I loved skating again!

For the first time in a year!

The exhibition that night found me happier than I had been in a long time.

I don't know yet what caused the sudden change. Part of it may have been escaping from the depression of the communist countries. More likely, it was that I had finally given the decision to the Lord, and I knew He wouldn't let me make a mistake.

I felt good about staying with the tour. I was glad I had "gutted it out" and skated well in spite of my attitude up until now.

Before going home, we stopped in Davos to see the Haslers once again. I sort of unloaded my questions in front of Mr. Hasler, told him about the struggle of the past year, and asked his advice. He wouldn't commit himself. Naturally, being an official of the International Skating Union, he wanted me to keep going as an amateur. Yet he saw the advantages of turning pro, too.

By the time I got home four days later, my mind was pretty well made up.

People don't really believe me when I say this, but the money was not a big factor one way or the other. If I didn't feel like skating, no one could have paid me enough to

Home scenes: the Nowicki kids' awards in our family room (above), *and Mom making yet another outfit* (right).

make me go through another year like I'd just endured. I had to come to the point of knowing that the Lord wanted me to keep skating, and that He would help me enjoy it and share His love through it.

In fact, money has never been a big goal in our family. Reporters have often asked my folks over the years, "How much is all this costing you?" and they've run into a stone wall every time. My dad has said, "Look, I just don't want to talk about it. I don't want to discourage any other parent who's trying to raise a skating daughter."

Courtesy of the *Journal Star*, Peoria, Illinois

It's not that my family is rich or has had some secret fortune somewhere to pay for all my lessons, skates, and trips all over the world. My mom—in addition to everything else—took in sewing for three years before Grenoble, making skating outfits for other kids at the Wagon Wheel (she'd had lots of experience at that!). Then after dad bought the store in 1968, mom worked there up until Sapporo, doing everything from bookkeeping to delivering prescriptions.

And somehow, the Lord always helped us come up with the money. One night when we were watching the movies of my competitions, mom said, "Aren't you glad now that we ate hot dogs a few more meals so we could buy these?"

The negotiations began. The hardest part for me was to keep doing my weekend exhibitions and acting and talking like an amateur. One night in April, I was back in Troy, Ohio, to do a show, and I wrote:

Dear Lord,
    . . . Today I was thinking about turning professional and how a lot of people might think I'm contradictory from some things I've said in the papers how money isn't everything.
    Well, Lord, what are my pure motives for turning pro? What am I going to say to people who ask me—do I tell them only that I feel I don't want to be dependent so much anymore and that I feel it's Your will for me? Do I tell them the whole story of last year, etc.? Lord, until it's known that I am turning pro I ask that You will give me the sincere words to say that won't be letting anything be hinted at but won't be lying. That sounds too difficult for me, and it is. . . .
    Lord, take my worry away and replace it with peace and Your guidance. I need You and not confusion.

17
the dotted line

Meanwhile, things really began to happen in my family, too. Before leaving for Bratislava, I had gone into Carol's room one day when she was out. She was a sophomore now and getting more messed up all the time. She'd been elected a cheerleader, but after the second road trip she was told not to ride the team bus anymore.

I began to pray, "Lord . . . I'm worried about Carol. I asked You for a sister way back at the beginning, but now it's so hard for me to be a big sister to her. . . . Lord, I don't know how much she's drinking or what all she's getting into, and I'm worried. I just want her to be happy. Lord, please send an angel to be with her while I'm gone, and help her to turn around and find You."

Something inside me had wanted to open up to Carol, to share with her, and let her know I loved her. But I hadn't known how to go about it. We just weren't getting through to each other.

When I got home from tour, Carol was at O'Hare to meet me with the others. I noticed something different as soon as she didn't try to dodge the picture-posing like she'd always done before. She was even smiling.

There were swarms of people around, of course, and so we didn't get to talk on the bus to Rockford—except she managed to say, "Janet, I have to tell you something." It was just as busy once we got home; neighbors were over, and I was tired, and we eventually went to bed without talking.

The next morning when I got up, Carol was still sleeping—the folks had let her skip school since the night before had been so hectic and late. I went into her bedroom.

She woke up. I sat down on her bed and said, "I'm sorry we never got to talk yesterday. What did you want to tell me?"

She sat up. "Well, I have some bad news and then some good news. First, the bad news. You never really knew that last fall I was out drinking every weekend, most of the time both Saturday and Sunday nights. Remember that night when we came in while you and your friends were having a prayer meeting or something?"

I remembered.

"Janet, I'm really sorry about that. I bet you were really embarrassed. Anyway, here's the good news: While you were gone, I let Jesus Christ come into my life."

Fantastic! I hugged her. Then I asked how it happened.

She had been at a slumber party one night, and a friend of hers was there who had just become a Christian. The girls began talking about God, and this friend said something like, "Would you like for me to tell you guys what happened to me?" Everyone said yes.

So she began explaining how a person gets right with God. Carol told me, "Janet, I'd never realized that God was for me, too. I guess I thought He was just for people like you. But when this girl started talking and sounding like you—I knew He was for me, too." Carol had become a Christian that night.

The tension between us melted away. Before long, she

was filled with the Holy Spirit at one of the Thursday night prayer meetings at church. She was changed so much people even noticed it over the phone. She used to get tired of me getting all the calls—("Janet—it's for *you* again," all the time). Now, when I'd come to the phone, people would say, "Wow, something's happened to your sister!"

I began thinking about how important it was for Carol and all of us to follow Jesus alone, not other people. One day I came back after praying outdoors and wrote about it.

> I just went for a walk by Mrs. Kerns' house. It's a windy day but fresh and sunshiny. . . .
> As I was walking down the road, I thought how I would walk on the road of life, trying to follow the straight and narrow way of Jesus to His Father. As I go along, I want to grab on to people and tell them to . . . follow *me*? I said no—I'm not always going on the straight and narrow road all the time 'cause I'm human. It made me realize that I should have the attitude to take them by the hand for a while to get them in step with *Jesus,* the Leader, the Pied Piper, not me. I walk along behind Jesus *with* other people— not ahead of anyone. The line of followers on the path is continuous, but no one follows anyone else—everyone is following Jesus. His light is shining bright enough for all to see if they look toward Him.
> And then I was sitting on the bench just talking to my Lord, and my spirit also talked to my Lord by way of a gift. . . . I talked, and my spirit talked to God—and God talked to me!

My times of praying in a language of the Holy Spirit like that are probably not often enough. Whenever I do, I have the sense of really praising God adequately, like I could never do in English, and I'm sure that He especially appreciates that kind of communication.

In June I got out to Colorado for a week with the Lichtys, which was spiritual fellowship and sharing almost around the clock! We must have gone to a prayer meeting nearly every night.

Then it was back home for the signing of my professional contract. Dick Button had been working with International Management Inc., the company that manages the careers of people like Rod Laver, Jean-Claude Killy, and Arnold Palmer. Together, they had worked out a three-year contract for selected appearances (at least twenty-seven weeks out of the normal forty-two) with the Ice Follies for $1,455,000.

Which is a lot of money! Back in March *Sports Illustrated* had guessed that I "might get $100,000 a year right now if she signed with an ice show." But it really didn't faze me. The day I signed the contract in Chicago, I wasn't nervous at all—I just picked up my nineteen-cent ballpoint and wrote my name on a piece of paper. It was Dick and everyone else who were jittery and worried about everything going right.

It happened on a Tuesday afternoon in Arthur Wirtz's office (he owns the Black Hawks and Chicago Stadium, and started the Ice Follies years ago). There were all sorts of nice words about me now being the highest paid female athlete in the world, and all the TV specials, commercial deals, and movies that would probably be coming along soon. I made it clear that I kept the right to refuse any offer I didn't want to do for moral or any other reasons.

One reporter wanted to know how I would "avoid the vulgar commercialism of a Mark Spitz" (the Olympic gold medalist in swimming who's now sort of a show business sex symbol). Dick stepped up to handle that one for me by saying, "The difference is that Janet will be skating, whereas Mark isn't swimming."

But it wasn't long before I began to see a new danger. I was determined that I was going to be real in this circumstance just as I'd tried to be in all the others. About five weeks after the signing, I wrote:

> I really am starting to realize in a small way why Jesus said it's almost impossible for rich people to live in God's kingdom. It sounds crazy to think that if you have money

A publicity shot!

you won't love or trust God, but actually, it's true logically. Why should one trust God and Jesus for His will and love if it's possible to have everything *you* want with only money?

The thing is, we don't know what's best for us, and God does. Also, even though we have everything with money—it could be gone tomorrow. Jesus Christ is the *only* thing that's lasting. . . . Also, God has shown me that I can't do a thing like lose weight without trusting Him completely. I must keep my eyes on Him instead of food—or money.

It was really good for me to realize that my weight battle couldn't be solved by money. (In fact, it made it worse!) The Lord kept showing me, "You can't lose weight alone. You've tried so many times, and you've lost your determination so many times. Ask Me, and I'll help you, but you can't do it on your own." Every time I'd take the problem back and think I could handle it, I'd gain weight; every time I'd yield it to Him, I'd lose. It's just one more of the many areas of my life that He wants to bring under control.

About a week later, I wrote:

Lord, I'm giving You half my food money (I sent it to my church) . . . . I ask You to use it to feed others spiritually and by grace help me to look thin and *be* thin by Saturday. I guess it sounds like I'm bargaining. Lord, if You want to punish me for gaining weight by not helping me, You can. But I really *do* want to look good for *Your* glory—help me to know that this is all for Your glory *every day,* no matter what I'm doing . . . .

Lord, please guide me what to do with the money. It's all Yours—I want to use it for You—please guide me. . . .

There was one paragraph in the news release about my turning pro that was a little unusual. Before reporting to San Francisco to start rehearsing with the Ice Follies, "her first commitment is to make a nonpaid evangelical tour to Japan starting July 1st. Under the auspices of the Language Institute for Evangelism, an organization devoted to teaching English and the Gospel, she will attend open meetings in Tokyo, Sapporo, and Osaka to speak on how the Gospel has influenced her."

My New York agents had gulped a little at that and had worried that it would hurt my commercial value in Japan. (They even sent their Japanese agent to check out the crusade.) My response was simply to smile and say, "I'm going." I had one more thing I wanted to do before becoming a pro.

18
tour
without skates

Ken Wendling, the American missionary who heads up English Language Institute, had been in the United States the year before trying to rebuild a youth crusade for Tokyo. The singing group he had lined up had just canceled on him and all his plans had fallen through.

He was in Los Angeles one night praying, "Lord, what am I going to do? The auditoriums are all booked, and I don't have any program." That same night he was watching a Billy Graham special on TV when I came on. The light switched on in his head: "Janet Lynn—she's a Christian! . . . and who's more popular in Japan?"

When he got in touch with me, it was like an answer to prayer. I had been frustrated ever since the Olympics, wondering how God was going to use what had happened there. I kept getting all this Japanese fan mail telling me what a great skater I was, and I didn't have a way to tell these people what the real secret was.

So a week and a half after I signed my contract, my dad and I took off for Tokyo. It was the first extended trip he'd ever made with me—we hadn't been together that much in fifteen years.

When we arrived, Ken had things organized a little better than the last time I'd come to Japan, when I'd about gotten crushed in the mob. We went immediately into a press conference. The first question was, "Really, why are you coming to Japan?"

I said, "I've been frustrated since the Olympics by all the compliments I've gotten from Japanese fans, because I haven't been able to tell them the rest of the story of my skating. Everyone has heard about my slogan, 'Peace and Love,' but I haven't yet explained the source of my peace and love, which is Jesus Christ. He is the one who has given me the ability to skate and has helped me all along." I really got quite specific —it was kind of fun to just come right out and say it!

They asked other questions, such as, "Why did you turn professional?" and "How did you keep smiling after you fell during the Olympics?" which was, I found, especially impressive to the Japanese. Their culture includes a strong sense of personal pride and fear of embarrassment.

We found out later that some of the reporters had come all set to nail me about my contract, about being a "greedy capitalist," and all that, but I guess they decided not to say anything when the conference took the direction it did.

That night, many of the Christians of Tokyo gathered downtown in one of the largest churches for a mass prayer meeting. It was such a beautiful sight to see all these Oriental Christians packing out the building and praying together openly in a common bond. Tokyo alone has more than 2.6 million young people between fifteen and twenty-four, and we really felt the need to ask for the Lord's help in communicating with them.

The first public meeting, however, was scheduled for Sapporo. When I first saw the city, it seemed a lot more barren without the snow. We went back to Makomanai Stadium one afternoon. A flood of memories came over me. It was desolate now . . . weeds growing here and there. We began walking up to the top where the Olympic flame had burned so majestically.

I felt sad. I asked the Lord to show me some significance in the flame. He seemed to say that the flame, the symbol of the Olympics and all their excitement, was only temporary —it no longer burned here at Sapporo. But Christ and the Holy Spirit bring excitement into my life every day. I wouldn't be missing anything by not skating in the next Olympics.

We went to the indoor skating rink. Standing there looking at all the empty seats, I thought about how neat it would be to come back and skate again there for the Lord some day. I've dreamed a lot of times about putting together a Christian ice show—I don't know how it would work out, but it's an idea . . . .

The local missionary who was with us interrupted just then and said, "Janet, why don't you come back here some day and skate for the Lord?" Wow!

We went back to Room H2-53 in the Olympic Village, where I'd signed the wall the day we left. The family who lived there was really nice in welcoming us; in fact, the Sapporo TV station had arranged to do an interview there. My first scribbling was fading now, so they had me sign a newly painted wall.

Only I changed it this time. I wrote, "Peace, Love † Life in Jesus Christ, Janet Lynn."

There were almost three thousand people out to the evening meeting. Some of the local sponsors were a little confused; they had planned it as more of a secular night for Janet Lynn to talk to the people of Sapporo. They had several non-Christian musical groups there to perform, and the emcee himself was apparently not a Christian.

Paul Ariga, the really dynamic Japanese evangelist who normally was to speak after me every night, was given only five minutes. He went longer than that, though, and by the time he finished he had spelled out the entire gospel.

Then it was my turn. Paul translated for me. I shared my spiritual faith as best I could. When Paul gave an invitation for response, nearly two-thirds of the audience stood to receive Christ. He had me lead them in the prayer of repentance, which they repeated after me. Then local Christians went ahead with one-to-one counseling.

Back in Tokyo, we had eight meetings altogether, and the response was much the same—even on a sweltering Sunday afternoon, when twelve thousand came. I had written a whole collection of things in advance to use during my seven or eight minutes each meeting. For instance, I planned to use two Scriptures as an introduction:

> In one of His talks, Jesus said to the people, "I am the Light of the world. So if you follow Me, you won't be stumbling through the darkness, for living light will flood your path" *(John 8:12, Living Bible).*
>
> "You must love the Lord your God with all your heart, and with all your soul, and with all your mind. And you must love your neighbor just as much as you love yourself" *(Luke 10:27, Living Bible).*

Then I planned to say:

> These two passages explain how I try to live and how I have found peace and love in my life. I am glad that I can share part of my personal life with you as well as sharing my skating with you at the Olympics.
>
> Though I fell in the Olympics, I believe that God's living light was upon me, and that's why I could keep smiling. I was skating for two reasons: to show God how much I loved Him, and to express love to the people watching and hope that they would find love in my skating for them personally.
>
> I wish all Japanese people peace and love within their hearts and lives. Nothing pleases me more than to see people with a true everlasting peace and love in their lives. *Arigato, sayonara!* ("Thank you, good-by!")

The thing was, I never ended up saying what I had planned. It seemed like I would just start, and then while waiting for the translator to finish, the Lord would give me the next sentence, and we'd go on like that. And what came out was what He wanted, I could tell.

I started getting scared after about two meetings: *What if I don't trust the Lord enough?* I started realizing how

133

important my part was in the meetings, and I wanted to be so sure that I wasn't just getting up and spouting on my own. Overall, though, I've never felt the guidance of the Holy Spirit in speaking so much as in Japan.

It was really important to be led by the Spirit during the two or three afternoons when we held meetings at universities. There were about twenty-five hundred students out at Waseda University, and it was really tense because a Communist demonstration was going on right across the street.

The Continentals, a really good group from the States, sang for a while at first. Then I came on and began, for some reason, to talk about the Four Spiritual Laws. I ended up explaining all four of them and talking for almost thirty minutes!

But the Lord knew what He was doing, because as soon as I finished, a big group of students had to leave the meeting and never got to hear the evangelist. So what I had said was strategic.

The meeting closed with a question time. Some of the questions were really tough: "If Christ is so good and His truth is so wonderful, why does your country have a thing like the Watergate scandal?"

I had to explain that first of all, Christ is not an American, and the United States is not entirely Christian. I then said, "No nation is perfect. I expect imperfect things from an imperfect society, and Watergate is one of those things. Even so, I'm proud of my country for its good points, such as giving me freedom and letting me worship as I please."

One of the questions was downright weird: "In the Old Testament, when Moses saw the flame in the bush, don't you think that was a UFO?" I think I just said, "No"—and dropped it at that!

In the press conferences and on television, I was naturally asked all sorts of questions about my personal life. They asked about marriage plans, and I said I was still waiting for God to guide me. I wasn't dating anyone right then, and I explained that there are so many things I want to do and accomplish —things I believe God wants me to accomplish—that I really don't know how marriage fits into all that. I guess I wouldn't be badly disappointed if I never got married, but then, provided I really loved a guy who was a Christian, maybe it would be all right, too!

I probably got most fearful the day I had to speak to the Tokyo Foreign Correspondents' Club. There were journalists there from a lot of different countries, many with their wives, and other important people as well.

Linda Foxwell, a missionary's daughter who traveled with me, and I disappeared into the ladies' room. The word spread, and soon there was a steady line of ladies coming in to get autographs. Finally, I said, "Linda, I've just got to have some time alone to pray before I speak. What am I going to do?"

"I don't know," she said. "There's no way we can keep them from coming in."

"You know what? I'm going to pray that they stop coming," I said.

Linda just stared at me!

We began praying. I said, "Lord, You know I have to speak, and I just really need to talk to You right now. I ask that no more ladies will come through that door until we're finished . . . ." We must have prayed about four or five minutes, and the door didn't open once.

The split second we said, "Amen," a lady came in the door! Both Linda and I burst out laughing. The poor woman didn't know what to do—she thought we were laughing at her. She got an autograph and walked right back out again!

I wrote a few notes while eating, but my speech went off in a different direction. I began talking about skating and the discipline it requires. Eventually I moved into the discipline of the Christian life and the lessons I had learned at Sapporo and other places. By the end, I saw people with tears in their eyes, and I just sat down thinking, "Lord, that wasn't me! That had to be Your work."

We took the high-speed train to Osaka for the final rally. On the way, Linda and I got to talking about my weight. I'd been eating a lot, and I knew that I should be slim for costume fittings the minute I got back to California.

We talked about how eating can get to be a god—you actually get upset if you can't have something. She told about a

Christian woman she'd heard about who decided to think of all the food she shouldn't eat as a sacrifice to the Lord. Instead of wishing she could have it, she turned it over to Him. *Not* eating became a joy for her instead of eating. And she lost weight.

We prayed about that and a lot of other things for an hour that night. We told the Lord I needed to lose five pounds in five days.

He and I did it!

Before coming home, I spent a couple of days doing business with Calpis, a Japanese soft drink company. One of the producers told my dad, "You know, I used to be a Buddhist, but I'm not really much of anything now. I took in part of one of the crusade meetings the other night, and I was fairly impressed."

Dad told me about him, and the next day I got to talk to him. He eventually agreed to at least consider Christianity, and when I gave him a Japanese New Testament someone had given me, he promised to read it.

And then before I knew it, I was back in San Francisco. I felt like a klutz the first time I stepped on the ice—I hadn't skated in almost two months, the longest break I'd ever taken. But it was so much fun! It felt like the first two months after competition season, when you just mess around.

It was a riot—no more school figures! I was finally free to concentrate on putting love into my skating every minute.

I summed up my feelings at the end of a letter I wrote to be sent to fans:

> I know I will miss my friends from my amateur years in skating, but I hope this new phase of my life won't end any friendships I already have . . . . Please realize that I'm still me, even though I'm a so-called professional now. I love people, I love skating, and, most of all, I love God.
>
> May the Lord bless you in your easy and hard times, in your joy and sadness, and in your mountains and valleys!
>
> Peace and Love and Life in Jesus Christ!